DATE DUE

GAYLORD			PRINTED IN U.S.A.

THE CALIPHATE

THE
CALIPHATE

BY

SIR THOMAS W. ARNOLD, C.I.E., Litt.D.

With a concluding chapter by
SYLVIA G. HAIM

LONDON
ROUTLEDGE & KEGAN PAUL LTD

First published in Oxford
at the Clarendon Press in 1924
Reissued with an additional chapter in 1965
by Routledge & Kegan Paul Ltd
Broadway House, 68–74 Carter Lane
London E.C.4
Printed in Great Britain
by Butler & Tanner Ltd
Frome and London

Reprinted 1967

PREFACE

THE following pages are based on lectures delivered in the University of London; the publication of them has been delayed owing to the exacting nature of the author's work in the School of Oriental Studies. Students of Muslim history will at once recognize his indebtedness to the works of Barthold, Becker, Caetani, Nallino, and Snouck Hurgronje, and he cannot claim to have done much more than present the result of their researches to English readers who may be unacquainted with the scattered writings of these distinguished authorities.

A part of Chapter IV has already appeared in the *Edinburgh Review*, and is reproduced here with the permission of the editor.

TABLE OF CONTENTS

I

THE CALIPHATE AND THE HOLY ROMAN EMPIRE

DURING the early part of the Middle Ages two rival political systems, one in the West and the other in the East, dwelt face to face, ignorant and entirely unappreciative of one another's ideals. Each claimed to exist by divine appointment and appealed for sanction of its authority to the revealed Word of God. When Pope Innocent III declared that the Lord had entrusted to Peter not only the Universal Church but the government of the whole world,[1] he enunciated that doctrine of a world religion which Christianity has held from its very inception; and the theory of the Holy Roman Empire set before it as its aim a World-State in which the Emperor would be universal sovereign, controlling and guiding the secular affairs of the faithful with an ever-widening authority, until it should embrace the whole surface of the globe. Similarly, Islam is a universal religion and claims the allegiance of all men and women, who must either accept the Muslim faith or pay tribute as subject peoples; corresponding to this common recognition of the same creed there was to be a unity of political organization in which all believers were to owe obedience to the supreme head of the community, the Khalīfah.

But in spite of these characteristics of resemblance the two systems were fundamentally different. The Holy Roman Empire was consciously and deliberately a revival of a pre-existing political institution that had been in existence before the birth of Christianity and was now revived under a specifically Christian character. Charlemagne assumed a title which had been held by heathen emperors before him, though the functions of his imperial office took upon themselves a specifically Christian character in consequence largely of his constant study of Saint Augustine's *De Civitate Dei*. But side by side with the Emperor was the Pope, and the Pope possessed spiritual authority and functions which were denied to the Emperor; as the Vicar of God upon earth, he ruled over and guided the souls of men, while it was the part of the Emperor to deal with the concerns of their bodies. As every student of the Holy Roman Empire knows, there was a long conflict over the problem of the true relationship between these two independent authorities; but throughout the centuries during which the Holy Roman Empire was a living force in Europe, the distinction between temporal and spiritual authority was never lost sight of.

The circumstances under which the Caliphate arose were entirely different. It grew up without any deliberate pre-vision, out of the circumstances of that vast empire which may almost be said to have been flung in the faces of the Arabs, to be picked up with the minimum of effort, by the rival empires of Persia and Rome, exhausted as they were by the age-long struggle in which they had endeavoured to tear one another to pieces, and in the case of the Roman empire, distracted by the acerbity of the theological antagonisms of rival Churches, still more embittered by racial antipathy. No one at the beginning of the seventh century, least of all an Arab, could have anticipated in imagination the vast extent, the immense wealth and power, which were to be under the control of the Successor of the Prophet when he reigned in Damascus or Baghdad. Unlike the Holy Roman Empire, the Caliphate was no deliberate imitation of a pre-existent form of civilization or political organization. It was the outgrowth of conditions that were entirely unfamiliar to the Arabs, and took upon itself a character that was exactly moulded by these conditions. The Caliphate as a political institution was thus the child of its age, and did not look upon itself as the revival of any political institution of an earlier date.

The theory as embodied in the works of Muhammadan theologians and jurists was elaborated in order to suit already operating facts ; the history of the development of this theory is obscure, but it certainly does not make its appearance in literature until after the Arab empire had become an accomplished reality. As we know it, this theory first finds expression in the Traditions, which claim to be the utterances of the Prophet

Muḥammad or his intimate companions. These Traditions, at first handed down only by word of mouth, were embodied in authoritative compilations during the third century of the Muhammadan era, and in all matters of dogma, religious observance, law and the practices of the devout life they were regarded as authorities second only to the Qur'ān itself. Indeed reverence for the Traditions reached such a point that their prescriptions were placed on a level with the sacred text of the Qur'ān, and so early as the end of the first century of the Muhammadan era it had been laid down that in arriving at a decision in regard to the meaning of the Qur'ān, the finding of the Traditions was decisive, and that it was not the Qur'ān which sat in judgement on the Traditions.[2] Thus it is impossible to appreciate the place which the Traditions occupy in Muslim thought unless due recognition is given to the unassailable authority which is assigned to them.

The word 'tradition' is a somewhat unsatisfactory translation for the Arabic 'Ḥadīth', as technically employed to mean a record of the actions and sayings of the Prophet, for in the Christian system of theology a tradition does not generally carry the same weight as a text from the revealed Word of God, and Christian tradition has not received verbal embodiment in the same rigid form as in Muhammadan literature;[3] for in Muslim theology a Ḥadīth is believed in many cases to represent the actual words of God, even as a verse of the Qur'ān is held to be the eternal Word of God; and if all the Traditions do not actually thus take the form of divine utterances, still they are regarded as having been divinely inspired in substance, if not in the actual form of their verbal expression. Thus they carry with them the sanction of divine authority and they serve, together with the Qur'ān itself, as one of the bases of religious doctrine, religious practice, and ritual observance, as well as being the source of political theory and law. European scholars have made it clear that many of these so-called Traditions of the Prophet were invented in the interests of some political party or theological sect, and even Muhammadan theologians themselves have frankly recognized the fact that some utterances claiming to be Traditions were really forgeries; but when the authoritative collections of Traditions, to which reference has already been made, were compiled in the third century, they were accepted without question and were held to admit of no cavil or dispute. Quite early in the Muhammadan era it became obvious that the various problems that faced the Muslim thinker, problems not only of the political order but also problems connected with the framing of systems of religious dogma and the settling of metaphysical controversies, could not be satisfactorily solved by reference merely to the Qur'ān, for they had never presented themselves to the primitive society to which the Qur'ān had been revealed. It was, therefore, necessary in a religious community that relied for guidance on the inspired Word of God, to have some settlements of these various difficulties, couched in a form of unimpeachable authority equal to that of the Qur'ān itself, if they were to win acceptance in the minds of the faithful. It was this intellectual and practical need that gave rise to the literature of the Traditions and claimed for them so unassailable a prerogative. Such Traditions as embodied the theory of the Caliphate were, therefore, to be received as matters of faith and could demand the unhesitating allegiance of the believer.

Apart from the question of its inception, the theory of the Caliphate differed in another important respect from that of the Holy Roman Empire. The orthodox Muslim world has never accepted the existence of any functionary corresponding to a Pope, though among the Shiahs an exalted degree of authority has been assigned to the Imām as an exponent of divine truth; but among the Sunnīs, to whom the historic Caliphate (the subject of the present inquiry) belongs, divine revelation is held to have ceased with the Qur'ān and the Traditions, and the task of interpretation of these sources of truth was assigned to the 'Ulamā (the learned) and did not belong to the Caliph. Thus the Caliph, as will be explained later, enjoyed no spiritual functions. As Imām he could lead the faithful in prayer, in acts of public worship; but this was a privilege which the meanest of his Muslim subjects could enjoy,* since for such an office no special ordination or consecration was required, and the performance of this religious activity implied the possession of no specific spiritual character, such as is connected with the doctrine of the Christian priesthood. Islam knows of no priesthood, of no body of men set apart for the performance of religious duties which the general body of the faithful are not authorized to perform. It is true that in Muhammadan society there are persons known as the 'Ulamā, who have given themselves up exclusively to the study of theology with a degree of self-sacrificing devotion that is worthy of all praise; but these men, as their designation indicates, are only 'the learned'; they are laymen and they receive reverence only because they have devoted themselves to the unceasing study of the Word of God and the divine law; nor have they been set apart for this form of activity by any distinct form of religious appointment, nor do they in any such manner acquire any religious or spiritual powers of operation, which would lift them to a higher stage in an ecclesiastical organization, if the Muslim religion possessed one. Moreover, for the punctual performance of public worship at the five prescribed periods of daily prayer, it has been found convenient to assign to any public Mosque an Imām, who is always present at such times and can lead the devotions of the

* A slave, a nomad from the desert, a callow youth, or the son of a prostitute may act as Imām.[4]

faithful. But such an Imām has no priestly character; he has not been ordained to this office by any higher ecclesiastical functionary; he is a layman, just like the members of his congregation, but since their daily avocations in the world would not always admit of their regular attendance, it is found convenient to employ a man who is not hampered by such ties; but any one of his congregation could at any time take his place and, as adequately, perform all the prescribed ritual observances and satisfy all the demands of the religious law. Much misunderstanding has arisen from the failure to recognize all the implications connected with the absence of a priesthood in Islam. Familiarity with Christian doctrine and Christian ecclesiastical systems has caused observers to view Muslim society and Muslim institutions from a point of view familiar to themselves but entirely foreign to that of the Muslim world. The Muslim doctrine of the nature of God and the explanation of the Divine attributes as being utterly unlike and distinct from human attributes, implies a relation between man and his Creator entirely different from that taught by a system of dogma embodying the doctrine of the Incarnation. The divine nature is so absolutely unrelated to, and so far removed from, human nature, that (according to orthodox Muslim teaching at least) no single man can claim to be nearer to God than his fellows; all believers are alike, in their utter subjection to the unapproachable divine majesty.[5]

Accordingly, in the Muslim world there is not that separation between Church and State which has been a source of so much controversy in Christendom. It is true that the Muslim 'Ulamā have often denounced the unrighteous ways of the Caliph and his government, and have demanded for the religious law an extensive operation which the officers of government have generally refused to grant; but these have been matters of dispute, not between a priesthood and the civil authorities, but between individual laymen and other laymen. For the understanding of the status of the Caliph, it is important therefore to recognize that he is pre-eminently a political functionary, and though he may perform religious functions, these functions do not imply the possession of any spiritual powers setting him thereby apart from the rest of the faithful.

In one other respect does the Caliphate differ from the Holy Roman Empire. The Holy Roman Empire is dead; in reality it had perished long before Napoleon in 1806 declared that he would no longer recognize the existence of it, and Francis II invented for himself the new title of Emperor of Austria. There is no monarch left who makes any pretension to be the successor of Charlemagne, nor is any defence any longer put forward for the political theory on which the institution of the Holy Roman Empire was based. But the case is very different in the Muhammadan world. There are still rival claimants for the

B

possession of the title of Caliph, and the theory of the Caliphate is still cherished by theological students who shut their eyes to the altered circumstances of the political world, and expound the doctrine of the Caliphate as though they were still living in the ninth century.

II

ORIGIN OF THE CALIPHATE. THE TITLES OF THE CALIPH

THE Prophet Muḥammad nominated no successor. It would be idle to speculate why with his genius for organization he neglected to make such provision for the future of the new religious community he had founded. His health had been failing for some time before his final illness, and perhaps, like Oliver Cromwell, he was 'so discomposed in body or mind, that he could not attend to that matter'.[1] It is more probable that he was a child of his age, and fully realized the strength of Arab tribal feeling, which recognized no hereditary principle in its primitive forms of political life, and left the members of the tribe entirely free to select their own leader.

As soon as the news of his death reached the ears of his most faithful followers and earliest converts, Abū Bakr, 'Umar and Abū Ubaydah, they immediately took action to secure the election of Abū Bakr, in accordance doubtless with plans they had matured in anticipation of the approaching death of the founder of their faith.[2] Hearing that some of the chiefs of the Banū Khazraj, the most numerous tribe in Medina that supported the Muslim cause, were holding a meeting to elect a chief, they hurried to the house in which this meeting was being held, and after some discussion the election of Abū Bakr was carried by acclamation. Apparently very few persons were present at this meeting, and when on the following morning Abū Bakr took his seat on the Minbar in the Mosque where the dead Prophet had been accustomed to address his followers, 'Umar called upon the faithful to swear allegiance to Abū Bakr, and those who had been present at the meeting the night before, renewed the oath of allegiance they had then made, and the rest of the assembly followed their example.

We have here an exemplification of the ancient Arab custom, in accordance with which, when the chief of a tribe died, his office passed to that member of the tribe who enjoyed the greatest influence, the leading members of the tribe selecting to fill the vacant place some one among themselves who was respected on account of age, or influence, or for his good services to the common weal ; there was no complicated or formal method of election, nor within such small social groups would any elaborate procedure be necessary, and when the choice of a successor had been made, those present swore allegiance to him, one after another, clasping him by the hand.

Abū Bakr was sixty years of age when he was elected to succeed the Prophet, and he enjoyed the dignity for two years only. According to the tradition recorded by Muslim historians, Abū Bakr nominated 'Umar as his successor. But actually during the Caliphate of Abū Bakr, 'Umar had been the virtual ruler, and he assumed the functions of head of the state immediately after Abū Bakr's death without any formality. This again was quite in accordance with primitive Arab custom, when the prominent position of any particular individual clearly marked him out as the ultimate successor of the head of the tribe; but though no formalities might be necessary, it was virtually by election that such a man would take the place of the dead chief, and the rest of the tribe would express their assent by swearing allegiance to him.

When ten years later 'Umar had received a mortal wound at the hand of an assassin, he is said to have appointed a body of electors, six in number, to choose a successor. Doubt has been cast on the truth of this story, and there is reason for thinking that 'Umar, like the Prophet Muḥammad himself, left the matter entirely in the hands of those concerned.[3]

The greatest living historian of Islam, Prince Caetani, has suggested that this story of 'Umar having nominated a body of electors was an invention of later times, in order to justify the practice that prevailed during the Abbasid period, of first having a private proclamation of the Caliph in the presence of the magnates of the empire, at which they swore allegiance to the new sovereign, and then following it up by the public proclamation, in which the populace received the communication of the election and gave assent by acclamation.[4] However this may have been, there was certainly some form of election in the case of the first four Caliphs—Abū Bakr, ʿUmar, ʿUthmān, and ʿAlī; in neither instance was there any question of hereditary succession, nor was the choice of either of these Caliphs influenced by considerations of relationship.

As will be shown later on, in the theory of the Caliphate, the fiction of an election was always kept up, and, in the opinion of the Sunnī legists, the Caliphate was always an elective office, and they accordingly lay down rules as to the qualifications of the electors. Even up to modern times there are survivals, under the Ottoman Sultanate, of this primitive form of the institution.

In 661 the office of the Caliphate passed into the hands of Muʿāwiyah, the founder of the Umayyad dynasty. Muʿāwiyah was the first to establish the hereditary principle, and in 676 (four years before his death) he nominated his son Yazīd as his successor. Deputations from the chief cities in the empire came to Damascus, and took the oath of allegiance to Yazīd. When Syria and ʿIraq had thus paid homage to the heir apparent, the Caliph took his son with him to the holy cities of Medina and Mecca, and compelled the citizens there to accept this innovation, though in the face of considerable opposition.

The precedent thus established was generally followed in later times throughout the Abbasid period also. The reigning Caliph proclaimed as his successor the most competent of his sons, or his favourite son if affection or prejudice influenced his choice, or the best qualified of his kinsmen. The oath of allegiance was then paid to this prince as heir apparent, first in the capital, and then throughout the other cities of the empire. But the direct succession of father and son was so little exemplified in actual practice in the case of the first twenty-four Caliphs of the Abbasid dynasty, that for a period of more than two centuries (754–974) only six of them were succeeded by a son. When the power of the Abbasid Caliphate had sunk into insignificance, it became more common for son to succeed father, but throughout the whole period political theory maintained that the office was elective.

Before going into the details of the theory, it will be convenient to complete this historical survey of the institution of the Caliphate. The establishment of the Umayyad dynasty, with its capital in Damascus, marked a distinct breach with the pious tradition of the original converts to Islam, whose interest was rather in Islam as a body of doctrine and a code of practice, than as a political organization. One of the most illuminating discoveries made by modern historians in regard to Muslim history is the recognition of the fact that the enormous expansion of Islam in the second half of the seventh century, was not the result of a great religious movement stimulated by a proselytizing zeal for the conversion of souls, but was an expansion of the Arab tribes, breaking through the frontiers which their powerful neighbours in the Roman and Persian Empires had grown too weak to defend. It has been made clear that religious interests entered but little into the consciousness of these conquering Arab armies which overran Syria, Palestine, Mesopotamia, and Persia, for this expansion of the Arab race was rather the migration of a vigorous and energetic people driven, by hunger and want, to leave their inhospitable deserts which had become impoverished through increasing desiccation, and overrun the richer lands of the more fortunate neighbours.[5]

So long as the central government remained in Medina, Islamic influences were predominant, and the faithful Companions of the Prophet could attempt to organize the new society in accordance with the teaching of their dead master. But when in 661 Mu'āwiyah made Damascus the capital of the empire, the old heathen sentiment of the Arabs was able to assert itself. In place of the theoretical equality of all believers in the brotherhood of Islam, we find the Arabs asserting themselves as a dominant aristocracy ruling over subject peoples. They exhibit as much pride of race and boast as much of their genealogies as in the old heathen days before Islam came to condemn such vainglorious vanities. During the whole of the Umayyad period, pious circles in Mecca and Medina which clung to the primitive apostolic traditions felt that Mu'āwiyah instead of preserving the piety and primitive simplicity of the Prophet and his Companions, had transformed the Caliphate into a temporal sovereignty, animated by worldly motives and characterized by luxury and self-indulgence. The Umayyads were accused of having secularized the supreme power in the very midst of Islam, and of having exploited the inheritance of the Muslim community for the benefit of the members of their own tribe and family. This breach of sentiment between the centres of Muslim orthodoxy and the capital of the Arab empire is of importance for the student of the development of Muslim political theory. For though the political theory of the Caliphate could not entirely ignore the actual facts of history, yet it was in Medina especially that Islamic speculation of all kinds—theological, legal, and political—had its beginning, and at the outset such theories were worked out without any reference to actual living fact. This is the reason why so much of Muhammadan law is purely theoretic in its character, and lays down many principles that have hardly ever been put into practice. While Mu'āwiyah, with his genius for administration, and his skill and tact in dealing with the haughty aristocracy out of which he had himself sprung, was laying the foundations of a great empire, the theorists—jurists as well as theologians—were elaborating in Medina the principles of the laws that were to govern the Muslim community, and were framing systems that had very little to do with the actual life of their co-religionists.

The unprejudiced student of history can realize how unjust was the judgement which these theorists, and the historians of the Abbasid period who accepted their point of view, passed upon the Umayyads ; they were under the delusion that the life of a simple and patriarchal religious society such as the Companions of Muḥammad had lived in Medina, could be reproduced in a vast empire that had absorbed countries accustomed to the civilized administrative methods of the Roman world ; they could not recognize that the larger sphere of activity such as primitive Muslim society during the life-time of the Prophet never dreamt of, demanded methods of administration and organization, for which the inspired Word of God provided no guidance.

Before the Umayyad dynasty came to an end, the Caliph in Damascus ruled over a vast empire stretching from India and the borders of China in the east, to the shores of the Atlantic and North Africa in the west—comprising all the territories of the old Persian empire and the eastern provinces of the Roman empire (with the exception of Asia Minor)—and his generals after conquering Spain, had even sent troops north of the Pyrenees. It was from the greatness of this empire, and the riches and power it had brought to the head of the State, that the title of Khalīfah derived its secular grandeur. At the outset this title merely implied succession to the Prophet Muḥammad. As according to Muslim theology, Muḥammad was the last of the prophets,[6] of course the prophetic office ceased with him, and no one of his successors could lay claim to speak as the mouthpiece of divine revelation. But for the community that acknowledged him as their head, Muḥammad had been ruler, judge, administrator, preacher, and leader of public worship—and these functions were held to have passed on to his successors, and acquired an added glory and magnificence with each brilliant success of the Arab arms.

Under the new dynasty of the Abbasids the Persian converts had come to the front, and the transference of the capital from Syria to Mesopotamia, and ultimately in 762 to Baghdad, marks the recognition by the new dynasty of its reliance upon its Persian supporters, and consequently the chief offices of state came to be held by men of Persian origin. Whereas the symbols of Umayyad rule had been the sceptre and the seal, under the Abbasids increased emphasis was laid on the religious character of their dignity, and the mark of their exalted office became the mantle of the Prophet. This sacred relic was worn by the Abbasid Caliph on the day of his succession when his subjects first took the oath of allegiance to him, and on every ceremonial occasion, as when, for example, he appeared in the Mosque to lead the prayer in public worship. Theologians and men of learning (which in Muslim society means pre-eminently religious learning) received a welcome in the Abbasid Court such as they had never enjoyed under the Umayyads. The precepts of the religious law were zealously upheld by the head of the government and by the officers of state appointed by him, and all branches of learning connected with religious dogma and law received a great impetus under the generous patronage of the Khalīfah. Several of the Abbasid Caliphs took pleasure in being present at religious discussions, invited men of learning to their court, and had a theological education imparted to their sons. At the same time they showed their spirit of orthodoxy by the persecution of heretics.

This emphasis laid on religious considerations re-acted on the status of the Khalīfah himself, and increased emphasis came to be laid on the title ‘ Imām ’. This title first appears on coins and inscriptions in the reign of Ma’mūn (813–833) and various traditional utterances (to which reference will be made later on) ascribed to the Prophet, in regard to the obedience due to the Imām, are significant of the added dignity with which this title had become invested. Such injunctions of obedience were made all the more impressive by another characteristic of the Abbasid court, which distinguished it from the more patriarchal spirit of the Umayyad court, namely, the presence of the executioner by the side of the throne. The Umayyads, as true Arabs, retained something of the frank intercourse of the desert, and would condescend, on occasion, to bandy words with their subjects; but approach to the Abbasid Caliph was hedged round with more pomp and ceremony, and by his throne stood the sinister figure of the executioner, with a strip of leather to catch the blood of the victim. Summary executions became characteristic of the administrative methods of the Abbasids, and many a man summoned in haste to the Palace took the precaution of carrying his shroud with him. The elaboration of Court etiquette which developed alongside with this autocratic exercise of authority, tended further to enhance the awe with which the office of Khalīfah was regarded, for the Abbasids adopted the servile ritual of the old Persian court and made their subjects kiss the ground before them, or in the case of higher officials, or more favoured personages, permission was given either to kiss the Caliph's hand or foot, or the edge of his robe.

It was under such circumstances connected with the increasing extension and wealth of the Arab Empire that the theory of the Caliphate was elaborated. None of the authoritative statements of this theory appear to belong to the primitive period of Muslim history, though the date at which they attained their final expression is uncertain. But certain technical terms connected with this supreme office are certainly of an early date, e. g. when, after the death of Muḥammad in 632, it became necessary to invent some official designation for the new leader of the community Abū Bakr gave orders that he should be described by the modest title of 'Khalīfah Rasūl Allāh' (successor of the Apostle of God). In this haphazard manner originated the title which was to describe the ruler of one of the greatest empires the world has ever seen.

The Prophet had been at one and the same time head of the State and head of the Church. The paramount control of political policy was in his hands; he received the ambassadors who brought the submission of the various Arab tribes, and he appointed officers to collect dues and taxes. He exercised supreme authority in military matters and the dispatch of military expeditions. He was at the same time supreme legislator, and not only promulgated legal statutes but sat in judgement to decide cases, and against his decision there was no appeal. In addition to the performance of these offices of the administrative and political order as ruler, general, and judge, he was also revered as the inspired Prophet of God and the religious dogmas he enunciated were accepted by his followers as revelations of divine truth, in regard to which there could be no doubt or dispute. At the same time he performed the highest ecclesiastical functions, and as Imām led the prayer in public worship at the canonical hours in the Mosque of Medina. In all these respects Abū Bakr was a successor of the founder of the faith—with the exception of the exercise of the prophetic function, which was held to have ceased with the death of the Prophet. The choice of the designation 'Successor' was doubtless prompted by a genuine feeling of humility on Abū Bakr's part, in the difficult days when the existence of the young Muslim community was threatened, and when it might still have appeared to some observers to be doomed to extinction owing to the death of its founder. There is no evidence that Muḥammad in his promulgation of the Qur'ān ever contemplated the possibility of the word Khalīfah becoming a title of his successor, nor is it likely that it was any use of this word in the Qur'ān itself which suggested to Abū Bakr that he should style himself 'the Successor of the Apostle of God'. That this simple title of Successor, or Khalīfah, should have acquired so much dignity is due to the rapid extension of the Arab conquests and to the enormous wealth and power which these conquests brought to the rulers of the newly established empire.

There were two other titles that have been commonly associated with the title Khalīfah. The Caliph 'Umar, who succeeded Abū Bakr in 634, was at the outset of his reign first styled 'Khalīfah of the Khalīfah of the Apostle of God', but soon, as this designation was recognized to be too long and clumsy, he decided to be called 'Khalīfah' simply, and it is from 'Umar's reign, the period of the great conquests, that this simple title begins to attain so much significance. But 'Umar was the first to assume the other title of 'Amīr ul-Mu'minīn' (the Commander of the Faithful). This was obviously a more arrogant designation, and ‘Umar is said at first to have hesitated to allow himself to be addressed by a title that appeared to be so vainglorious, though the title was not a new one and had been held by ‘Abdullāh ibn Jaḥsh, one of the early converts of Muḥammad, who was killed in the battle of Uhud, in the third year of the Ḥijrah, it having been bestowed upon him after his successful raid at Nakhlah in the previous year.[7] This insignificant personage is said to have been the first to have been so styled, though tradition has sometimes ascribed it to others,[8] but for the head of the Muslim community to assume such a title gave it an entirely different significance, and the constantly reiterated statement in the Qur'ān that power (Amr) belongs to God alone might well have caused the pious soul of ‘Umar to shrink from so presumptuous a designation; moreover the word Amīr, much less the phrase, Amīr ul-Mu'minīn, unlike the titles Khalīfah and Imām, does not occur anywhere in the Qur'ān at all. But after ‘Umar had once adopted it, it became one of the commonest titles of his successors, and the rare instances in which other Muslim princes have ventured to arrogate it to themselves have generally been significant of an attempt to shake off allegiance to the head of the Muslim community and claim independence of the generally recognized Caliphate.

It was by this title, Amīr ul-Mu'minīn, that the Caliph was commonly known to Christian Europe during the Middle Ages, under such strange forms as: ‘Elmiram mommini’, ‘Miralomin’, ‘Mirmumnus’, &c.

In its assumption of authority this title was characteristic of the immense power which the Caliphate had achieved during the reign of ‘Umar. His armies tore from the Roman empire some of its fairest provinces in the East, annexed the fertile land of Egypt, and pushed their way westward along the coast of North Africa; they overran Palestine and Syria, and after crushing the armies of the Persian king, established Arab rule over practically the whole of the old Persian empire, until they reached the banks of the Oxus in the extreme north east.

While the title of ‘Amīr ul-Mu’minīn’ emphasized the secular aspect of the high position of the Caliph, a third title, that of ‘Imām’, had special reference to his religious function as leader of the faithful in public worship. The word occurs frequently in the Qur’ān as meaning a leader, a guide, an example, model, &c., e. g., in chap. ii, verse 118, where God says to Abraham, ‘I will make thee a leader for men,’ and in xxi. 73, God speaking of Isaac and Jacob, says ‘And we made them leaders who should guide (men) by our command’; again in xxv. 74, the righteous are represented as saying ‘O Lord, . . . make us examples to those who fear Thee’, and in xvii. 73, God describes the Day of Judgement as ‘The Day when we shall summon all men with their leader’. The word is used not only of a person, but also of a thing, such as an inspired book, e. g. in xi. 20, and xl. 11, the Book of Moses is described as ‘ A guide (imām) and a mercy ’. How little the later orthodox use of the word ‘ Imām ’, whether in its wider sense as meaning any leader of public worship or in its more restricted reference to the supreme head of the Muslim community, was anticipated in the Qur’ān, may be recognized by the fact that it is used in the Qur’ān not only to describe the prophets of God and other devout personages, but unbelievers also, as in ix. 12, where God says ‘ Fight against the leaders of infidelity ’ ; and in chapter xv, where reference is made to the destruction of Sodom and another evil city, God says ‘ We took vengeance upon them and they both became a manifest example (imām) ’ (xv. 79). It is strange that the word ‘ Imām ’ nowhere appears in the Qur’ān in its common signification of a leader of public worship. As is well known, it is customary in the Muslim world in the ritual observance of public worship at the five canonical times appointed for the daily prayers, for the believers to stand in rows behind a conductor, called the ‘ Imām ’, and this ‘ Imām ’ standing by himself in front of them all, performs the various ritual movements of bowing, kneeling, and prostration, while the rest follow his example, and bow, or kneel, or touch the ground with their foreheads at the same time as he does. As the leader of the Muslim community, Muḥammad was accustomed during the whole of the ten years of his life in Medina to act in this manner as Imām, and lead the public worship for his followers; it was only when he was absent from Medina on some military expedition that he delegated this office to one of his followers, whom he nominated for this express purpose; they were mostly obscure persons, and the name of a blind man who is said to have thus officiated for as many as thirteen times has remained quite unknown to us, as no historian appears to have thought it worth while to put it on record. The fact that during Muḥammad's last illness, while he himself was in the sacred city, Abū Bakr was ordered to lead the public worship in the mosque in his stead, facilitated his election as the Prophet's successor, because leadership in prayer had been one of the most obvious and frequently recurring indications of the position that Muḥammad held as head of the new social order, at once political and religious.[9]

After Muḥammad's death, one Khalīfah after another continued to perform this office, and this leadership in public worship was looked upon as a symbol of leadership generally. As the Arab dominions expanded, and provincial governors were dispatched to assume authority over newly annexed territories, one of the first public functions that a governor would perform was to appear in the mosque and take his place at the head of the assembled company of believers as leader of divine worship. With this public function was closely connected another institution which has an interesting history and an important place in the institution of the Caliphate. In early Arab society the judge sat upon a seat called a ‘ Minbar ’ and thence delivered his judgements. The word ‘ Minbar ’ has survived to the present day and now indicates the pulpit in a mosque ; but during the lifetime of Muḥammad and in the primitive Muslim society of Medina, the mosque was not only a place of prayer, but was the equivalent of the Roman forum—the centre of the political and social life of the community. In the mosque at Medina, the Prophet received the submission of the various Arab tribes who sent ambassadors to swear allegiance to him, and in the mosque he conducted all the business of state, from the ‘ Minbar ’. He not only gave instructions to his followers in matters of dogma and religious observance, but made political pronouncements also.

This association of the mosque with political life, and of the Minbar with the seat of authority of the ruler, did not disappear with the death of the Prophet. It was from the Minbar in Medina that the Caliph ‘Umar read out before the assembled congregation the announcement of a disastrous check to the progress of the Muslim armies in Persia, and made an appeal for volunteers. It was from the Minbar too that his successor, the Caliph ‘Uthmān, delivered a speech defending himself against the attacks brought against his methods of administration.

Further, there are several recorded instances of a newly-appointed governor of a province making a declaration of policy from the Minbar, after he had for the first time publicly assumed office by leading the congregation in worship. But as time went on, the Caliphs gradually discontinued this practice, and other symbols of the exercise of authority came more into evidence.

In connexion with the Minbar there is another technical term of some importance, the Khuṭbah, the address that is delivered to the congregation from the Minbar at the time of public worship as is the practice at the present day and has been for many centuries past, particularly on Fridays. In pre-Muslim days the Khaṭīb was the orator of the Arab tribe, who acted as judge in primitive Arabian society, and the utterance he made from the seat of authority was the 'Khuṭbah'. The 'Khuṭbah', in the mouth of Muḥammad, was often a political pronouncement, and might almost in some instances be described as a speech from the throne. After his death, as the boundaries of Muslim territory became extended and a provincial governor would have his own Minbar from which to address the assembled congregation, his 'Khuṭbah' might likewise bear the character of a political speech, but of course it would not carry the same importance as the Khuṭbah uttered by the supreme head of the community. Owing to a number of circumstances, the Khuṭbah gradually came to lose much of its original meaning and importance. Whereas in Medina, when the Muslim community was in its infancy, there was only one mosque and one Minbar, and only one person who pronounced the Khuṭbah, namely the Prophet himself—on the other hand, as the Arab empire grew, so the number of mosques increased, and the Khuṭbah could no longer be an address to the whole body of the faithful, for persons of slight political importance had on occasion to lead the prayer in public worship, and the Umayyad Caliphs themselves grew weary of this particular method of announcing their will to their subjects. The introduction of administrative methods copied from those of the provincial organization of the Roman empire, whose provinces had passed under Arab rule, made this form of verbal communication of the decisions and orders of the government, clumsy and unnecessary. Just as the Minbar gradually ceased to represent the throne of the monarch, or the seat of the judge, and became a mere pulpit, so the Khuṭbah, by a similar process of evolution, took on the character of a sermon or a bidding-prayer, repeated by any one who happened to be the Imām of the mosque. In modern times and for many centuries past, the Khuṭbah has largely consisted of ascription of praise and glory to God, and the invoking of blessings upon the Prophet, his descendants and companions; but it has retained something of its primitive political importance inasmuch as it generally includes also a prayer for the reigning sovereign, and the substitution in the Khuṭbah of a new name may announce the accession of a new monarch, or the transference of authority from one government to another ; e. g. when Ghāzān Khān, the Mongol Sultan of Persia, in 1300 withdrew his troops from Damascus and this city once again passed into the possession of the Mamlūk government of Egypt, the Khuṭbah in the great mosque was read in the name of Sultan Nāṣir and of the Khalīfah, after all mention of them had been intermitted for a hundred days.[10] One of the signs of sovereignty in the Muhammadan state has always been the inclusion of the name of the reigning prince in the Khuṭbah, pronounced by the Imām in the course of the congregational worship on Fridays and the great festivals, and on various occasions throughout the course of Muslim history, there have been such dramatic instances of the substitution of one name for another, as indicating a recognition of a change of government. It has also in more recent days been sometimes a matter of perplexity to European governments, as to how far they should allow or should forbid the name of a reigning Muslim monarch to be mentioned in the Khuṭbah of their Muhammadan subjects.

The early Caliphs could be described by either one of these three titles—Khalīfah, Amīr ul-Mu'minīn, and Imām. Each was a title of one and the same personage, but Khalīfah emphasized his relation to the founder of the faith, 'The

Apostle of God,' and put forward this apostolic succession as a claim for the obedience of the faithful; the second title, 'Amīr ul-Mu'minīn,' asserted more distinctively the authority of the ruler as supreme war lord and head of the civil administration; the third, 'Imām,' emphasized rather the religious activity of the head of the state as performing a certain definite religious function. This last title—Imām—is the favourite designation for the head of the Church among the Shiahs, since they lay special emphasis on the sacrosanct character of the successors of the Prophet, to whom they gradually attributed mysterious and almost supernatural powers, until, as at present, they came to believe in a hidden Imām who, unseen by men, guides and directs the faithful upon earth. Though the doctrine of the Imām was of no less importance in Sunnī theology, and though Imām was an official description of the Sunnī Khalīfah, it was not so favourite a designation with the Sunnīs as with the Shiahs, and it was probably under the influence of Shiah opinion that the Abbasid Caliph, Ma'mūn (813–833), was the first to put the title 'Imām' on his coins and inscriptions. The coins of his predecessors had generally borne the title 'Amīr ul-Mu'minīn'. It was also no doubt owing to the hieratic character that the institution of the Caliphate assumed under the Abbasids, that this ecclesiastical title 'Imām' came to be inserted on the coins of Ma'mūn, and in this practice he was followed by succeeding Abbasids.

Some differentiation between these various appellations may be recognized in cases where pretenders have arrogated to themselves one or other of the three, e. g. it was not until Abu'l-'Abbas as-Saffāḥ (afterwards the first Caliph of the Abbasid dynasty) had broken out into open revolt that he assumed the title of Amīr ul-Mu'minīn; his brother, Ibrāhīm, who had been regarded as leader of the Abbasid party before him, was known only as the Imām. Similarly, at a later period, in Western Africa, when the Shiah movement had won a large number of adherents from among the Berbers, their leaders were styled Imām, and it was not until 'Ubaydullāh, the ancestor of the Fatimid Caliphs, was proclaimed Khalīfah in Qayrawān in the year 909, that he assumed the title of Amīr ul-Mu'minīn. The latter title emphasizes the aspect of secular authority, whereas that of Imām indicates rather the status of the ruler in the religious order.[11]

III

THEOLOGICAL SANCTION FOR THE CALIPHATE IN THE QUR'ĀN AND THE TRADITIONS

WHEN the Muslim theologians began to search the Qur'ān for warrant for the use of these titles, they found, as has already been pointed out, no justification whatsoever for the use of Amīr ul-Mu'minīn, very little for that of Imām, and certainly none at all for the connotations that had already become connected with this word; and though the word Khalīfah and other words with a cognate meaning and derived from the same Arabic root occur constantly, yet in no instance is there any clear and definite anticipation of the technical use of the term so common in later Muhammadan theological and political literature. But just as the theologians and statesmen of medieval Europe appealed to the Bible in support of both Papal and Imperial claims, so the theologians and jurists of the Muslim world sought for some support of the political theory of the Caliphate in the revealed Word of God, and for them the authority of the Qur'ān was a matter of still greater weight and importance, since by theory the Qur'ān was the primary basis for law, both religious and civil. Many of the verses in which the term occurs were incapable of any interpretation directly connecting them with the political institution they were to defend, since the reference to Successor (Khalīfah) or Successors (Khalā'if, Khulafā) was made in general terms, and clearly had no reference to one single exalted individual. Such was the case in the following verses, 'God has promised to those among you who believe and work righteousness, that God will make them successors upon the earth, even as He made those who were before them successors, and that He will establish for them their religion which is pleasing to them, and that after their fear He will give them security in exchange' (xxiv. 54); 'It is He (God) who has made you successors (Khalā'if) on the earth, and has raised some of you above others by (various) grades in order that He may test you by His gifts' (vi. 165). Here the reference appears to be to the general mass of believers, who are 'successors' as entering into the inheritance of their forefathers. A similar use of the word 'successor' is made with a narrower reference when in the Qur'ān (vii. 67, 72) God reproaches an idolatrous tribe ('Ād), who rejected the message of the Prophet He had sent to them; this Prophet (Hūd) says to his fellow tribesmen: 'Marvel ye that a warning is given to you from your Lord through one of yourselves, that He may warn you? But remember that He made you successors after the people of Noah and increased you in tallness of stature' (vii. 67). Here, clearly, all that is meant is that the people of this tribe succeeded to the blessings enjoyed by the people of Noah before them. A few verses further on

(vii. 72) another prophet (Ṣāliḥ) whose message of divine truth was likewise rejected by his fellow tribesmen, the tribe of Thamūd, appeals to these unbelieving Arabs to recognize the blessings that God has conferred upon them. 'And remember that He made you successors of 'Ād and gave you dwellings in the land, so that ye build castles on its plains and hew out houses in the mountain. Then remember the benefits of God and do not do evil in the land.' Here again the reference is to a number of persons, and the word 'Khalīfah' cannot be explained in connexion with the historic Caliph, the supreme head of the Muslim community.

But there are two passages in which we find an individual reference, in each instance to a distinguished personage. In the first case it is Adam, and in the second David; these two verses from the Word of God have been quoted and discussed by generations of Muslim writers on the Caliphate, in order to emphasize their distinctive doctrine of the nature of this institution. The verse in which reference is made to David is the simpler of the two. 'O David, verily we have made thee a successor (Khalīfah) in the land; then judge between men with the truth, and follow not thy desires, lest they cause thee to err from the path of God' (xxxviii. 25). In the other passage God is represented as announcing to the angels his intention to create Adam. 'When thy Lord said to the angels, Verily I am about to place on the earth a successor (Khalīfah), they said, Wilt thou place there one who will make mischief therein and shed blood ? ' (ii. 28).

These two verses have produced volumes of commentary. It would seem that the word ' Khalīfah ' means here something more than mere ' successor ', though some commentators say that when God declared his intention of creating Adam, He called him a Khalīfah, a successor, because Adam was to be the successor of the angels who used to live upon earth before the creation of man. But other Muslim authorities interpret ' Khalīfah ' as meaning a vicegerent, a deputy, a substitute—a successor in the sense of one who succeeds to some high function, and they accordingly explain that Adam and David are given the designation of ' Khalīfah ' since each was on earth a vicegerent of God, in their guidance of men and in the warnings they gave as to the commands of God. It is obvious that such an interpretation could be employed to enhance the dignity and authority of the Caliph.

For a more clear and definite exposition of the political theory of the Caliphate it was necessary to appeal to the Traditions, and it was these Traditions that served as the basis of the systematic treatment of the doctrine of the Caliphate, which we find in the writings of the Muhammadan theologians and jurists. As explained above, it is impossible to assign an exact date for the earliest appearance of these Traditions, but there is no doubt that they were put forward in justification of the political institution that had gained acceptance with the main body of the faithful, and that the theory, in the main, grew out of the facts, and represents the crystallization of opinion in the minds of the supporters of the Sunnī Caliphate during the course of the first two centuries of the Muhammadan era. But it is important to remember that, though the critical investigations of European scholars have set out in a clear light the tendencious character of many of the Traditions, such an origin was entirely unsuspected by pious Muslims, and no such critical considerations entered into their minds, to shake their faith in the divine sanction which the Traditions provided.

Too much emphasis cannot be laid on the fact that law and political theory are considered in the Muslim world to be as much derived from divine revelation as religious dogma is. European writers are apt to lose sight of this fact, because they are accustomed to systems of law that are not derived from the same source as statements of Christian doctrine, for Roman law was in existence before the rise of Christianity, and though it was absorbed into the structure of Christian civilization, as were also the political institutions of the Barbarians who overran the Roman empire, still the political institutions derived from these sources were clearly recognized to have had an origin independent of, and prior to, the revealed documents on which the Christian Creed is based. But in Islam the case is quite different, for from the Qur'ān proceed dogma and law alike, and the jurist as well as the theologian takes as the foundation stone of his system first the Qur'ān and next the Traditions, and explains in cases of doubtful interpretation the former by means of the latter. Consequently the legist in dealing with the subject of the Caliphate can regard it as a divinely appointed institution and look to God's revelation in the Traditions for guidance in his account of it.

The Traditions clearly state that the Caliph must be a member of the tribe of the Quraysh, to which the Prophet himself belonged, and this qualification was fulfilled throughout the whole of the historical period considered above, in the persons of the Umayyad and Abbasid Caliphs, as it was also in the case of their Shiah rivals, the Fatimids of Egypt. This principle is variously laid down as follows: 'The Imāms shall be of the Quraysh'; [1] 'There shall always be a ruler over men from among the Quraysh'; [2] 'The Khalīfah shall be of the Quraysh, judicial authority shall be in the hands of the Auxiliaries, and the call to prayer with the Abyssinians'; [3] 'The Imāms shall be of the Quraysh; the righteous of them, rulers over the righteous among them, and the wicked of them, rulers over the wicked among them'.[4]

The Caliphate thus recognized was a despotism which placed unrestricted power in the hands of the ruler and demanded unhesitating obedience from his subjects. This autocratic character of the Muslim Caliphate was probably an inheritance from the Persian monarchy, into the possession of whose dominions the Muslim community had entered; for pre-Islamic Arab society had never known any such form of political institution, nor was it in harmony with the Qur'ānic doctrine of the equality of all believers or with that attitude of independence which marked the relations between the first Caliphs and the Arabs who had so recently come out of the desert. For we now find an uncompromising doctrine of civic obedience taught in one Tradition after another, e. g. 'The Apostle of God said: Whoso obeys me, obeys God, and whoso rebels against me, rebels against God; whoso obeys the ruler, obeys me; and whoso rebels against the ruler, rebels against me'.[5] 'The Apostle of God said: After me will come rulers; render them your obedience, for the ruler is like a shield wherewith a man protects himself; if they are righteous and rule you well, they shall have their reward; but if they do evil and rule you ill, then punishment will fall upon them and you will be quit of it, for they are responsible for you, but you have no responsibility.'[6] 'Obey your rulers whatever may hap, for if they bid you do anything different to what I have taught you, they shall be punished for it and you will be rewarded for your obedience; and if they bid you do anything different to what I have taught you, the responsibility is theirs and you are quit of it.

When you meet God (on the day of judgement), say, "O Lord, Thou didst send us Prophets and we obeyed them by Thy permission, and you set over us Caliphs and we obeyed them by Thy permission, and our rulers gave us orders and we obeyed them for Thy sake"; and God will answer, "Ye speak the truth; theirs is the responsibility and you are quit of it".' [7] 'The Prophet said: Obey every ruler (Amīr), pray behind every Imām and insult none of my Companions.' [8]

It was not merely the Caliph, but any lawfully constituted authority whatsoever, that was to receive the obedience of the subject, for in one Tradition the Prophet is reported as saying: 'O men, obey God, even though He set over you as your ruler a mutilated Abyssinian slave.' [9]

The political theory thus enunciated appears to imply that all earthly authority is by divine appointment, the duty of the subjects is to obey, whether the ruler is just or unjust, for responsibility rests with God, and the only satisfaction that the subjects can feel is that God will punish the unjust ruler for his wicked deeds, even as he will reward the righteous monarch. Such a doctrine seems also to be implied in the following Tradition in which the Prophet says: 'When God wishes good for a people, He sets over them the forbearing and wise, and places their goods in the hands of generous rulers; but when God wishes evil for a people, He sets over them the witless and base and entrusts their goods to avaricious rulers.' [10]

Further, in a Tradition in which the Prophet was represented as foretelling the future of the Muslim community and the troubles that would immediately precede the appearance of Antichrist, he says: 'When in those days you see the Caliphate of God upon earth, attach yourself closely to it, even though it may consume your body and rob you of your property.' Again: 'If the government is just, it may expect reward from God and the subjects ought to show their gratitude to it; if it is unjust, it incurs the guilt of sin, but the subjects must give proof of their support.'

The exalted position with which the Caliph was thus endowed and the hieratic character assigned to his office was still further emphasized by another designation, which makes its appearance at an early period, viz. Shadow of God upon earth. Whatever exaggerated interpretation the flatterers of a later age might give to this phrase, its primitive signification was that the protection which the temporal power afforded was just like the protection which God himself gives to men. The shadow of God, of course, originally meant the shadow provided by God, not the shadow which God in any anthropomorphic sense Himself cast. The word 'shadow' here is equivalent in meaning to a 'place of refuge', for just as in the shade a man may find protection from the blazing heat of the sun, so a government may ward off harm from its subjects.[11] In later times more mysterious meanings undoubtedly attached themselves to the phrase, as when a rebel, brought before Mutawakkil in 849, addressed the Caliph as the rope stretched between God and His creatures.[12]

A similar exaltation of his office was implied when the Caliph came to be styled ‘ Khalīfah of Allāh ’. Abū Bakr is said to have protested against being so addressed,[13] maintaining that he was only Khalīfah of the Apostle of God. Though this designation occurs as early as the year 656 in an elegy which the poet Ḥassān ibn Thābit,[14] a contemporary of the Prophet, wrote on the death of the Caliph ‘Uthmān, in this primitive period it was probably taken to mean only ‘ the Successor of the Prophet of (i.e. approved by) God ’, and it was probably only as the empire became enriched and the ceremonial surrounding the Caliph became more stately and pompous, that the phrase was taken to mean the Lieutenant or Substitute or Vicegerent of God; and more than one theologian protested against the use of it[15] on the ground that only one who is dead or absent can have a successor, and God of course can never be supposed to be in either of these conditions.[16]

Under the Abbasids it became quite a common appellation, and even the second Caliph of this dynasty, Manṣūr, in a Khuṭbah in the year 775 had declared that he was the power (sulṭān) of God upon His earth.[17] But under his successors the commoner phrase ‘ Khalīfah of God ’ became a mere convention. From the Abbasids this title was adopted, as will be shown later on, by many princes in succeeding centuries who arrogated to themselves the title of the Caliph after the break-up of the Abbasid empire.

The tendencious character of some of the Traditions appears clearly in those which exalt the Abbasids to the discredit of the Umayyads, such as: 'The Apostle of God saw the children of al-Ḥakam ibn Abi'l-'Aṣ * leaping upon his Minbar with the leap of apes, and this grieved him, and he never brought himself to smile until his death.' Again, the Prophet is represented as saying: 'I saw in a vision the children of Marwān taking possession of my Minbar one after another, and this grieved me, and I saw the children of 'Abbās taking possession of my Minbar one after another and that gladdened me.' Again: 'The children of 'Abbās shall reign two days for every one in which the children of Umayyah shall reign, and two months for every month.' [18]

Such Traditions certainly appear to be the invention of some political pamphleteer who wished to bring the Umayyad dynasty into contempt. There are also Traditions which prophecy that the Caliphate would remain in the possession of the Abbasids until they resigned it into the hands of Jesus or of the Mahdī; e.g. 'The Caliphate shall abide among the children of my paternal

* The ancestor of all the Caliphs of the Umayyad dynasty, with the exception of the first three.

uncle ('Abbās) and of the race of my father until they deliver it unto the Messiah.'[19] Further, the Prophet is represented as having said to 'Abbās: 'When thy children shall inhabit the Sawād (the alluvial plain of 'Irāq) and clothe themselves in black and their followers shall be the children of Khurāsān, the government shall not cease to abide with them until they resign it into the hands of Jesus, the son of Mary.'[20] Such Traditions indicate clearly how the theory grew up out of the actual historic facts; they were quoted in support of what had become a despotism, though in spite of its autocratic character it still retained some show of the earlier political institution of election.

In one respect only was the arbitrary, autocratic power of the Caliph limited, in that he, just as every other Muslim, was obliged to submit to the ordinances of the Sharī'ah, or law of Islam. This limitation arose from the peculiar character of Muslim law as being primarily (in theory at least) derived from the inspired Word of God, and as laying down regulations for the conduct of every department of human life, and thus leaving no room for the distinction that arose in Christendom between canon law and the law of the state.

The law being thus of divine origin demanded the obedience even of the Caliph himself, and theoretically at least the administration of the state was supposed to be brought into harmony with the dictates of the sacred law.[21] It is true that by theory the Caliph could be a Mujtahid, that is an authority on law, but the legal decisions of a Mujtahid are limited to interpretation of the law in its application to such particular problems as may from time to time arise, and he is thus in no sense a creator of new legislation. Further, this particular activity was hardly assumed by any of the Caliphs, probably largely in consequence of the indifference of most of the Umayyads to religious problems which they left to professed theologians, and by the time the Abbasids had come into power, the 'Ulamā had made good their claim to be the only authoritative exponents of the law.

IV

HISTORICAL SURVEY OF THE ABBASID DYNASTY

In the year 750, after the defeat of the Umayyads in the battle of the Zāb, the headship of the Muhammadan world passed into the hands of the Abbasids, and for five centuries each successive Caliph was a member of this family. As the name indicates, the Abbasids claimed descent from 'Abbās, the uncle of the Prophet, and were able to magnify their office by this claim to relationship with the founder of the faith. Their rise to power and their overthrow of the Umayyads was the result of a number of circumstances, the most important of which were the following. The Shiah party which upheld the claims of the family of 'Alī to the Caliphate, had on more than one occasion broken into open revolt, and had never ceased secretly to foster dissatisfaction towards Umayyad rule. The Shiahs were the legitimists of Islam; they claimed that 'Alī, the cousin and son-in-law of Muḥammad, was the only rightful successor of the Prophet, and that after his death, by right of succession, the Caliphate should have passed to his descendants, and the descendants of his wife Fāṭima, daughter of the Prophet. In their schemes for the destruction of Umayyad rule, the Abbasids allied themselves with the Shiahs, pretending a common devotion to the 'Family of the Prophet'—a phrase which to the Shiahs meant the descendants of 'Alī, while the Abbasids applied it to the descendants of the Prophet's uncle. After the Abbasids had achieved success and had got all the help they wanted from the Shiahs, they, without hesitation, threw them over, and even persecuted those members of the Shiah party whom they deemed dangerous to the stability of their rule.

Considerable sympathy for the Shiah cause had been felt in Persia, and the Persians had a further grievance against the Umayyads in that though the Persians had embraced Islam, the Umayyads had kept them in a condition of humiliation and had refused to them that recognition of equality which was their right, in accordance with the doctrines of the faith. The Abbasids thus came into power largely in consequence of their claim to be the defenders of the faith, and partly through their support of the family of the Prophet as against the representatives of the old pagan Arab aristocracy that had usurped the throne. This loyalty to the faith they showed by their vindication of the claims of the converts and of the children of converts to an equal place in Muslim society along with those Arabs whose pride of race had hitherto led them to disregard the Islamic ideal of the brotherhood of all believers.

The change from the Umayyad to the Abbasid dynasty was thus the substitution of a Muslim rule for an Arab kingdom. Under the Umayyads Arab nationality had been predominant; the habits and usages of the old heathen Arab culture before the rise of Islam had flourished unchecked. The Umayyad Caliph had distributed his favours among the members of the Arab aristocracy to the exclusion of others, and the narrow tribal sympathy which was shown by the members of the reigning house was one of the circumstances that weakened their authority and paved the way for the revolt of the Abbasids.

It was under the Abbasids that the decline of the empire set in. The year 800, the date of the coronation of Charlemagne in Rome and the establishment of the Holy Roman Empire, may be taken as the culminating point of the prosperity of the Abbasid empire, though a prince of the Umayyad family, who had fled to Spain, had already made that country a separate kingdom in 756, and North Africa from 800 practically became an independent kingdom under the governor who founded the Aghlabid dynasty and made his post hereditary in his family. One province after another rapidly made itself independent, Egypt and Syria were cut off from the empire, and separate dynasties were established in Persia. By the tenth century the authority of the Abbasid Caliph hardly extended beyond the precincts of the city of Baghdad, and the Caliph himself was at the mercy of his foreign troops, for the most part of Turkish origin, lawless and undisciplined. The Caliph Muqtadir (908–932) was twice deposed, and at the end of an inglorious reign, marked by drunkenness, sensuality, and extravagance, was killed in a skirmish with the troops of one of his generals ; his head was stuck upon a spear, and his body left lying on the ground where he fell.

The degradation to which the Caliphate had sunk during this reign was signalized by the great schism which established a rival Caliphate in the Sunnī Church. Up to this period the Umayyad rulers of Spain had made no attempt to claim for themselves that headship of the Muslim world which their ancestors in Damascus had enjoyed during the great days of the Arab conquests, and had contented themselves with such titles as 'Amīr', 'Sulṭān', or 'Son of the Khalīfah'. But now the great 'Abd ur-Raḥmān III, who during his long reign brought Muslim Spain to a loftier position than it had ever enjoyed before, decided himself to assume the title which the Abbasids in Baghdad appeared no longer worthy to hold. Accordingly, in the year 928 he ordered that in the public prayer and on all official documents he should be styled 'Khalīfah' and 'Commander of the Faithful'. He might well have looked with pity and contempt upon Muqtadir, the representative of the rival house, who still continued in Baghdad to use such high-sounding titles.

After the death of Muqtadir, his brother Qāhir was elected to succeed him, but after a reign of terror of two years he was deposed, and his eyes were blinded with red-hot needles. He was tortured to induce him to reveal the place where his treasures were hidden, and remaining obstinate in his refusal, was thrown into prison and kept there for eleven years. After his release he was seen begging for alms in a mosque in utter destitution, though his own nephew sat upon the throne. The conspirators set up in his place Rāḍī, a son of the murdered Muqtadir, and for seven years he was the helpless tool of powerful ministers, 'having nothing of the Caliphate but the name', as a Muhammadan historian puts it. He is said to have been the last of the Caliphs to deliver a Khuṭbah at the Friday prayer. On his death in 940 he was succeeded by his brother, Muttaqī, another son of Muqtadir. But a few months later a revolt of the Turkish mercenaries compelled Muttaqī to flee from his capital and take refuge in Mosil, where he sought the protection of the great Hamdānid princes, Sayf ud-Dawlah and Nāṣir ud-Dawlah, who in their brilliant courts in Mosil and Aleppo extended a generous patronage to Arabic poets and men of letters. These two brothers were renowned for their splendid military achievements, and they restored the fugitive Caliph to his capital; but there they had soon to leave him, in order to look after affairs in their own dominions.

Another conspiracy compelled the unfortunate Caliph to flee from Baghdad a second time, and after fruitless appeals to various Muslim princes for assistance, he rashly placed himself in the hands of the Turkish general, Tūzūn, who had been the cause of many of his troubles. Though Tūzūn at first received him with all marks of outward respect, he subsequently blinded the Caliph with a hot iron and compelled him to abdicate. Tūzūn then set up another puppet Caliph, Mustakfī. In the following year Tūzūn died, but the Caliph only passed from the hands of one master to another, for he was presently compelled to welcome in his capital the Buwayhids, who in their victorious progress southward from Persia challenged the authority of the Turkish troops that had for so long terrorized the population of Mesopotamia. The Buwayhid prince feigned respect for the Caliph Mustakfī, and received from him titles of honour ; but the real power rested with the new conquerors of the Muslim capital, and presently Mustakfī too was blinded.

Thus there were at one and the same time three Abbasid princes living, who had held the high office of the Caliphate, all cruelly blinded, all robbed of their wealth, and in their blindness dependent upon charity or such meagre allowance as the new ruler cared to dole out to them. Henceforth, the history of the Abbasids assumed a new character ; for during the next two centuries the Caliphate became entirely subordinate to some powerful and independent dynasty that thought to add to its prestige by taking the helpless Caliphs under its protection. The first of these dynasties was that of the Buwayhids, already mentioned. They were a Persian family who took their rise in the north of Persia and gradually extended their authority southwards, until in 945 their troops entered Baghdad. For more than a century the authority of the Buwayhids was paramount in Baghdad and the Caliphs were merely tools in their hands, set upon the throne, or deposed, according to the will of their captors. Humiliating as the position was, it was rendered all the more galling by the fact that the Buwayhids were Shiahs, and therefore did not really recognize the claim of the Sunnī Khalīfah to the supreme headship of the Islamic world. They were the first princes who insisted on having their names mentioned in the Khuṭbah along with that of the Caliph—a practice that afterwards became common as the Caliph ceased to exercise effective authority.

Aḥmad, the youngest of the three Buwayhid brothers, but the real conqueror, contented himself with the humble title of Mu'izz ud-Dawlah (' Strengthener of the State '), while his brothers, 'Alī and Ḥasan, were designated respectively 'Imād ud-Dawlah (' Pillar of the State ') and Rukn ud-Dawlah (' Prop of the State '). But under this pretended show of submission, Mu'izz ud-Dawlah did not hesitate to exert his authority whenever stern measures seemed called for. In less than a fortnight after he had taken the oath of allegiance to the Caliph, he was alarmed by rumours of a plot directed against his own authority, and accordingly resolved to depose the Caliph. Going to the palace of Mustakfī, who was on that day to receive an ambassador in solemn audience, he kissed the ground before the throne; he then kissed the Caliph's hand, and remained standing for a while before him talking. When he had taken his seat two of his officers came forward, and the Caliph, thinking that they too wished to kiss his hand, stretched it out to them; but they pulled him ignominiously from his throne, twisted his turban round his neck, and dragged him along the ground to the palace of Mu'izz ud-Dawlah, where he was kept a prisoner and his eyes were put out.

His cousin, Muṭī', was set upon the throne of the Caliphate in his place, but though he held the office for twenty-eight years (946–974) he was a mere cipher in the state, and living on a scanty pension might well complain that nothing was left to him but the Khuṭbah, the bidding prayer in which his name was mentioned during the Friday service.[1] But even this last symbol of his exalted office might be taken away. Ṭā'i', the successor to Muṭī', fell out with the Buwayhid prince, 'Aḍud ud-Dawlah ('The Arm, or Support, of the State'), son of the eldest of the three Buwayhid brothers mentioned above. In revenge this prince caused the Caliph's name to be omitted from the Khuṭbah in Baghdad and other cities for two whole months. But even though the actual power of the Caliph was thus reduced to zero and he became a mere puppet in the hands of his Buwayhid master, the same pomp and show were observed on ceremonial occasions, when it was considered necessary to impress on men's minds the majesty and dignity of his exalted office.

Under 'Aḍud ud-Dawlah, who had inflicted such humiliation upon the Caliph, the Buwayhid kingdom reached the culmination of its greatness. Before his death in 983 he had become master of all the lands from the Caspian Sea to the Persian Gulf, and from Ispahan to the borders of Syria. While his father was still alive, he had already given vent to his ambitious schemes by taking advantage of the difficulties into which his cousin, Bakhtiyār, had fallen in 'Iraq on account of the insubordination of his Turkish mercenaries, and he had occupied Baghdad in 975, rescued his cousin, but afterwards threw him into prison and seized his lands. Hereupon 'Aḍud ud-Dawlah's father interfered and insisted on the release of Bakhtiyār and the restoration to him of his dominions; but the breach between the two cousins naturally continued, and 'Aḍud ud-Dawlah showed his vindictiveness in every possible way. The Arab historians tell a long story of his having robbed his cousin of a favourite Turkish page-boy, the loss of whom appears to have reduced Bakhtiyār almost to a state of imbecility, so that he shut himself up and refused to eat, spending his time in weeping, even neglecting the most important function of an oriental monarch, in that period, of giving public audience at court. In the following year, on the death of his father, 'Aḍud ud-Dawlah again attacked his cousin, defeated him and put him to death. 'Aḍud ud-Dawlah thus became master of 'Iraq and overlord of the helpless Caliph in Baghdad.

It has been necessary to make this excursion into the troubled politics of the Buwayhid family in order to illustrate the position that the Caliph still held in the economy of the Muslim State in spite of his entire lack of political power. In order to celebrate his victory, 'Aḍud ud-Dawlah made use of the Caliph, Ṭā'i', as his instrument for his own glorification. Since by theory the Caliph was still head of the whole Muslim world and the fountain of honour, if 'Aḍud ud-Dawlah had invented some new dignity for himself, public sentiment would not have been impressed. Accordingly the Caliph, doubtless much against his will, conferred upon 'Aḍud ud-Dawlah a robe of honour, like that of a sultan; crowned him with a jewelled crown, and bestowed upon him other insignia of royal rank—bracelet, collar, and sword—and presented him with two banners, one of them decked with silver such as was carried before an Amīr, and the other decked with gold such as was carried before the heir apparent. What was the whole purpose of 'Aḍud ud-Dawlah in making the captive Caliph bestow on him such an unusual honour is not quite clear. Such a banner had never before been given to any one not belonging to the imperial family, and it would seem to indicate that 'Aḍud ud-Dawlah contemplated the ultimate seizure of the Caliphate for himself. A diploma of investiture as heir apparent had also been drawn up, and to the horror of the courtiers it was read aloud. This was a breach of the etiquette of the court, for on all previous occasions it had been the custom for such a diploma to be handed to the heir apparent unopened, and for the Caliph to declare: 'This is the diploma I have granted to you; take care that you act in accordance with it.'

But 'Aḍud ud-Dawlah was still not content, and in the following year he made a still further encroachment on the imperial prerogatives of the Caliph by compelling him to give orders that the drums should be sounded at the gate of the prince's palace three times in a day—morning, sunset, and nightfall—an honour that hitherto had been reserved exclusively for the Caliph himself. More than this, the Caliph even made a further concession by permitting the name of 'Aḍud ud-Dawlah to be inserted in the Khuṭbah and pronounced in the mosque on Friday. The insertion of the name of a monarch in the Khuṭbah was a symbol of the assumption of sovereignty, and it marks the lowest depths of degradation that the Caliphate in Baghdad had ever reached.

The infliction of such humiliations on the Caliph is in striking contrast with the honour and reverence paid to him, whenever it was politic to bring him forward, as the supreme head of the faith. In the very year after 'Aḍud ud-Dawlah had extorted the privileges above-mentioned, an ambassador was sent to Baghdad in 980 by the Fāṭimid Caliph of Egypt, 'Azīz bi'llāhi. He was received with impressive ceremonial: the troops were drawn up in serried ranks, and the nobles and officers of the state were arranged in order of their dignity in the place of audience, but the Caliph was invisible behind a curtain. When 'Aḍud ud-Dawlah received permission to approach, the curtain was raised, and the spectators could see the Caliph seated on a high throne surrounded by a hundred guards in magnificent apparel and with drawn swords. Before him was placed one of the most sacred relics in Islam—the Qur'ān of the Caliph 'Uthmān; on his shoulders hung the mantle of the Prophet; in his hands he held the staff of the Prophet, and he was girt with the sword of the 'Apostle of God'. 'Aḍud ud-Dawlah kissed the ground before this spectacle of imposing majesty, and the Egyptian envoy, awe-struck, asked him: 'What is this? Is this God Almighty?' 'Aḍud ud-Dawlah answered: 'This is the Khalīfah of God upon earth,' and he continued to move forward, seven times kissing the ground before the Caliph. Then Ṭā'i' ordered one of his attendants to lead him up to the foot of the throne. 'Aḍud ud-Dawlah continued to make a show of reverence before such unapproachable and impressive majesty, and the Caliph had to say to him: 'Draw near,' before he would come forward and kiss the Caliph's foot. Ṭā'i' stretched out his right hand to him and bade him be seated. 'Aḍud ud-Dawlah humbly asked to be excused, and only after repeated injunctions would he consent to sit down in the place assigned to him, after first reverently kissing it. After this elaborate ceremony, Ṭā'i' said: 'I entrust to you the charge of my subjects whom God has committed to me in the East and in the West, and the administration of all their concerns, with the exception of what appertains to my personal and private property. Do you, therefore, assume charge of them.' 'Aḍud ud-Dawlah answered: 'May God aid me in obedience and service to our Lord, the Commander of the Faithful.' This solemn farce ended with the bestowal of seven robes of honour upon 'Aḍud ud-Dawlah, who kissed the ground on the presentation of each, and then took his leave followed by all the rest of the great assembly.[2]

It is typical of the unreality that marks much of the history of the institution of the Caliphate from this time onwards, that 'Aḍud ud-Dawlah, as a Shiah, did not accept the claims of the Caliph before whom he made such a pretence of submission and reverential awe. But as an administrator, he had to deal with a Sunnī population which regarded the Caliph as Imām and as head of its faith, and like Napoleon he found it politic to make concessions to the religious prejudices of his subjects. He may also have wished to show the Egyptian ambassador that (though a Shiah) he rejected the claims of the Caliph in Cairo to be descended from Fāṭimah. The man who in this public manner had shown such signs of slavish respect to the majesty of the Caliph, was capable the very next year when returning to Baghdad from a journey, of so insulting the Caliph as to send a messenger bidding him come out of the city to meet him, and the helpless Tā'i' was unable to refuse, though it was unprecedented for the Caliph to go out of Baghdad to meet any one.

The Buwayhid tyranny continued throughout the next reign, that of Qādir (991–1031), and for the greater part of that of his son, Qā'im (1031–1075). Reduced to absolute insignificance these Caliphs could only look on helplessly while others, more powerful and strenuous, controlled the political life of the Muslim world, without any reference at all to the prince who claimed to be Commander of the Faithful. But in spite of the insignificance of the Abbasid Caliph in Baghdad, the Muslim world was not prepared to select another member of the tribe of the Quraysh, to take his place as head of the faithful, and the attempt made by the Amīr of Mecca, Abu 'l-Futūḥ, in 1011, to get himself so recognized, hardly deserves mention. The Fātimid Caliph of Egypt, Ḥākim, had put to death one of his Wazirs, and the son of the murdered man, in the hope of being able to take revenge for his father, fled to the powerful Bedouin tribe of the Ṭayy in Syria, and invited Abu 'l-Futūḥ to declare himself Caliph. The Amīr of Mecca fell in with the proposal, and after inducing the inhabitants of the Hijaz to take the oath of fealty to him, joined the Banū Ṭayy, taking with him such holy relics as the staff of the Prophet and the sword of ‘Alī. Though at first he received a warm welcome from this tribe, he soon recognized that the bribes of Ḥākim had more influence with them than his holy relics, and so he abandoned his project in the following year, and hastened back to Mecca, where his position was threatened by the ambitions of one of his relatives.[3]

V

THE EXPOSITION OF THE JURISTS

It was during this period of the degradation of the Caliphate that the earliest systematic treatise on the theory of this institution, that has been made accessible to the historical student, was compiled. Born in the reign of Ṭā'i', and dying at the age of eighty-six in the year 1058, in the reign of Qā'im, Māwardī saw the Caliphate at the lowest ebb of its degradation, and the theoretical character of his account of it is in striking contrast to the actual historic facts of the case. He was one of the most distinguished jurists of his day and held the office of judge in several cities, lastly in the capital, Baghdad, itself; besides a number of works on political theory, he wrote also a commentary on the Qur'ān. With an entire disregard for the facts of history during the four preceding centuries of the Muhammadan era, he maintains that the office of Caliph or Imām is elective, and he lays down as qualifications for the electors that they must be of good reputation and upright life; of the male sex and of full age; they must have knowledge of the qualities required in an Imām, and necessary insight and judgement for making a wise choice. In an ingenious manner he endeavours to make the theory of election fit in with what he knew to be the actual fact, viz. that almost every Caliph had nominated his successor. He states that authorities are not agreed as to the number of electors required to make an election valid, for some maintained that there must be unanimous agreement on the part of all duly qualified Muslims in every part of the Muslim world; obviously, such an electorate could never have acted under the conditions of life in that period; so he cites the election of Abū Bakr as evidence that those present at the time of the death of the former leader of the community, were sufficient to represent the whole body of the faithful. The question then arises as to the number of persons who could in such a case be permitted to represent the opinion of the whole community. In the election of Abū Bakr Māwardī states that it was five; before his death, ‘Umar appointed an electoral college of six; but other authorities were of opinion that three persons were sufficient, on the analogy that a contract of marriage may be drawn up by one person in the presence of two witnesses. Others, however, have held that an election might be announced by a single voice, and thus Māwardī arrives at the conclusion that each Caliph may appoint his own successor, and yet the elective character of the institution may be preserved.[1]

But before any one is eligible for election to this high office, he must possess the following qualifications: he must be a member of the tribe of the Quraysh; he must be of the male sex, of full age, of spotless character and be free from all physical or mental infirmity; he must have sufficient knowledge for the decision of difficult cases of law, and the sound judgement required for public administration, and he must show courage and energy in the defence of Muslim territory.

The Caliph must thus be a person capable of fulfilling administrative, judicial, and military functions. These functions Māwardī sets out in detail as follows: the defence and maintenance of religion, the decision of legal disputes, the protection of the territory of Islam, the punishment of wrong-doers, the provision of troops for guarding the frontiers, the waging of war (jihād) against those who refuse to accept Islam or submit to Muslim rule, the collection and organization of taxes, the payment of salaries and the administration of public funds, the appointment of competent officials, and lastly, personal attention to the details of government.[2] These varied activities expected of the Caliph, Māwardī sums up as being 'the defence of religion and the administration of the state'.

As explained above, Māwardī practically ignores the dependent position into which the Caliphate had sunk and the rise of independent Muslim states that disregarded its authority; but his distinguished contemporary, al-Berūnī, writing in the reign of Qā'im (1031–1075), with that exactitude of scientific observation which characterized his genius, frankly recognized the true nature of the situation, and stated that what was left in the hands of the Abbasid Caliph was only a matter that concerned religion and dogmatic belief, since he was not capable of exercising any authority in the affairs of the world whatsoever.[3]

A later writer of the twelfth century, Niẓāmī-i-'Arūḍī, who put forward much the same theory as Māwardī, found a place in it for the numerous independent monarchs that had arisen in dominions once forming part of the Caliphate. After explaining the nature of the prophetic office, he goes on to say that after the death of the Prophet he must assuredly require, in order to maintain his Law and Practice (sunnat), a vicegerent, who must needs be the most excellent of that community and the most perfect product of that age in order that he may maintain this Law and give effect to this Code (sunnat); and such a one is called an Imām. But this Imām cannot reach the horizons of the East, the West, the North, and the South in such wise that the effects of his care may extend alike to the most remote and the nearest, and his command and prohibition reach at once the intelligent and the ignorant. Therefore must he needs have lieutenants (nā'ibān) to act for him in distant parts of the world, and not every one of these will have such power that all mankind shall be compelled to acknowledge it. Hence there must be an administrator and compeller, which administrator and compeller is called a 'Monarch', that is to say, a king; and his vicarious function (niyābat) 'Sovereignty'. The king, therefore, is the lieutenant (nā'ib) of the

Imām, the Imām of the Prophet, and the Prophet of God (mighty and glorious is He !).[4]

In any study of the theoretic exposition of the doctrine of the Caliphate mention must be made of Ibn Khaldūn, one of the greatest thinkers that the Muhammadan world has produced, and it will be convenient to give his account of the doctrine here, though he belongs to a later period than has been reached in the preceding historical survey. Born in Tunis in 1332, he took an active part in the political life of his time in the service of one prince after another, until, in 1382, he settled in Egypt where he was made chief Qāḍī of the Mālikī school of law, and he died in Cairo in 1406. With encyclopaedic knowledge and a judgement sharpened by a wide and varied experience of affairs, he takes a broad survey of Muslim history and works out an attractive theory of the origin and development of human society and culture. He attached himself to no philosophic system, but relied upon revelation for final guidance in matters of belief. He lays it down that the most solid basis for an empire is religion, since man has been placed in the world to perform the duties imposed upon him by religion in preparation for the future life; in order that he may come to know the divine law, which will secure for him happiness in the next world, he must be guided by a Prophet, or one who takes the place of a Prophet, that is the Khalīfah. Whereas ordinary kingship is a human institution, and the laws made by a king are based only upon reason and have reference only to the well-being of men on earth, the Khalīfah guides men in accordance with the dictates of the religious law (shar'), the precepts of which always bear in mind their ultimate destiny in the world to come. Accordingly, Ibn Khaldūn bases the necessity of an Imām or Khalīfah on the religious law given by divine revelation, adding to it, in accordance with the commonly accepted doctrine of the Sunnī legists the concensus of the companions of the faith and their followers; and he rejects the opinion of those philosophers who put forward a rational basis for the necessity of an Imām and urge that men must have a leader, because civilized life is only possible in an ordered society. On the contrary, the Khalīfah exists by divine appointment, and God makes him His vicegerent in order to guide men to the good and turn them away from the evil. At the same time he attacks the Shiah doctrine that an Imāmate is one of the pillars of the faith, and rather takes a utilitarian view of this institution, as existing only for the general good and as having been entrusted to human agency. He defends at some length the principle that the Khalīfah must belong to the tribe of the Quraysh, not only on the theological grounds that the office would thus enjoy the blessing of God, since the Prophet himself had belonged to this tribe, and that God Himself had recognized that the tribe comprised persons who were capable of performing the difficult functions of a Khalīfah; but also on the basis of certain considerations of a purely historical character, e.g. the Quraysh being one of the most powerful and respected tribes of Arabia could assume leadership over the rest, and one member of the tribe, elevated to the exalted position of Imām, would have the support of a powerful body of men, linked to him by ties of relationship, and could thus, in spite of the separatist tendencies of the Arabs, form a centre for united political life and historical development. Unlike Māwardī, he recognized that as an institution the Caliphate had undergone considerable change during the course of the various dynasties which had upheld it.

At the outset (he says) the Caliphate was only a religious institution for guiding the faithful to the observance of the religious law; but under the Umayyads it took on the character of a secular monarchy, and its original religious character became inextricably mixed up with the despotic rule of the king, compelling obedience by the sword. As the power of the Abbasids declined, soon after the death of Hārūn ur-Rashīd, the essential features of the Caliphate gradually disappeared, until there remained nothing but the name. Now that power had passed out of the hands of the Arabs altogether, the Caliphate might be said to have ceased to exist, though sovereigns of non-Arab origin have continued to profess obedience to the Caliph out of a feeling of religious reverence.[5]

VI

RECOGNITION OF THE ABBASID CALIPHATE FROM THE ELEVENTH TO THE THIRTEENTH CENTURY

STILL throughout the whole period of the decline of the Caliphate up to the date of the death of Musta'ṣim (1258), the Caliph was to all orthodox Sunnis the Commander of the Faithful, and as Successor of the Prophet he was held to be the source of all authority and the fountain of honour. The Caliph by his very name led men's thoughts back to the founder of their faith, the promulgator of their system of sacred law, and represented to them the principle of established law and authority. Whatever shape the course of external events might take, the faith of the Sunnī theologians and legists in the doctrines expounded in their text-books remained unshaken, and even though the Caliph could not give an order outside his own palace, they still went on teaching the faithful that he was the supreme head of the whole body of Muslims. Accordingly, a diploma of investiture sent by the Caliph, or a title of honour conferred by him, would satisfy the demands of the religious law and tranquillize the tender consciences of the subjects of an independent prince, though the ruler himself might remain entirely autonomous and be under no obligation of obedience to the puppet Caliph.

To this strange political fiction there is a

parallel in the history of the Holy Roman Empire during the fifteenth century. While the unfortunate Emperor, Frederick III, having been driven out of Vienna, was wandering about from monastery to monastery as a beggar, making what money he could out of the fees paid by those on whom he conferred titles, a contemporary jurist, Aeneas Piccolomini (afterwards famous as Pope Pius II), could write that the power of the Emperor was eternal and incapable of diminution or injury, and that any one who denied that the Emperor was lord and monarch of the whole earth was a heretic, since his authority was ordained by Holy Writ and by the decree of the Church.[1] Similarly, the Caliph was still by theory the head of the Muslim state, and however much any other ruler might take power into his own hands, he might still find it politic to recognize the Caliph as the theoretical source of all authority. The Muslim legists continued to make such extravagant claims on behalf of the Caliph, even in the days of his deepest humiliation, and even the Buwayhids, though their occupation of Baghdad was the culmination of the rapid growth of their extensive dominions, and though the Caliph was their pensioner and practically a prisoner in their hands, found it politic to disguise their complete independence under a pretence of subserviency and to give a show of legitimacy to their rule by accepting titles from him. Quite a number of other princes followed their example. When Maḥmūd of

Ghazna at the close of the tenth century renounced his allegiance to the Sāmānid prince whom his father had served as a Turkish slave, he turned to the Abbasid Caliph, Qādir bi-llāh, in order that he might receive some justification for his rebellion. The Caliph bestowed upon him the high-sounding title of Yamīn ud-dawlah, Amīn ul-Millah, the friend of the Amīr ul-Mu'minīn.[2] Maḥmūd was one of the most powerful sovereigns of his day in the East, and he had no need of any support for his authority other than that of his own armies. The allegiance he professed to the Caliph was thus merely a recognition of the imperial authority of law.

From the year 945 till 1055 the Buwayhids had continued to appoint and depose Caliphs as they thought fit. The rise of a new power in Persia, the Saljūqs, destroyed the ascendency of the Buwayhids, and the guardianship of the Caliph passed into their hands. This new and vigorous Turkish race, which first appears in Muslim history at the beginning of the eleventh century, entered upon a career of conquest by which it built up an empire stretching in the days of its greatness from the Oxus and the Hindu-Kush to the Syrian shore of the Mediterranean in the west, and from the north of Persia to the borders of the Arabian desert in the south. The power of the Buwayhids declined before the rise of this new power, till the Saljūqs swept them away entirely, and when the Saljūq prince, Tughril, entered Baghdad in

1055, he was received as a deliverer and the Caliph conferred on him the title of 'Sultan of the East and the West'[3] (Appendix IV). The Caliphate passed under a new tutelage, but, in this case, not of so oppressive a character, since instead of being Shiahs as the Buwayhids had been, the Saljūqs were Sunnīs and accordingly revered the Caliph not merely out of political considerations, but as being the Khalīfah of God; but they assumed for themselves the designation 'Shadow of God', which had in former days been the prerogative of the Caliph only,[4] and they even robbed the Caliph, Mustarshid (1118–1135), of that sacred relic, the mantle of the Prophet, which was worn by the Caliphs on the occasion of their coronation and on other solemnities.[5] Under the protection of the Saljūqs, however, the position of the Abbasid Caliph improved, and when they fell out among themselves and became weakened by dynastic wars, the Caliph was able to regain something of his lost authority. Mustarshid even raised an army, and taking the field, ventured to march against his Saljūq overlord, Mas'ūd ibn Muḥammad ibn Malikshāh, the ruler of 'Iraq and Kurdistan. He made his way right up to Kirmanshah, and before the engagement in which he was defeated, he delivered after the Friday service a Khuṭbah which the historian declares 'in eloquence transcended the highest zenith of the sun and attained the height of the Heavenly Throne and the Supreme Paradise'. The bolder attitude which a Caliph could now take towards the family that had, for eighty years, kept the Caliphate in subserviency may be judged by the words: 'We entrusted our affairs to the house of Saljūq and they rebelled against us.' This attempt to achieve independence ended in disaster and the death of the Caliph. Still, as the authority of the Saljūqs declined, successive Caliphs repeated the attempt, and at last Nāṣir had the satisfaction of seeing the head of Tughril ibn Arslān, the last Saljūq ruler of Persia, exposed in front of his palace in Baghdad (1194).

But this short-lived flicker of independence was soon to be followed by the crowning disaster of a Mongol invasion, when, in 1258, the army of Hūlāgū captured Baghdad and put the Caliph Musta'ṣim to death.

The awe with which the institution of the Caliphate was regarded even in these days of its weakness,* may be realized by the fact that, cruel and bloodthirsty savage though Hūlāgū was, even he hesitated to put to death the successor of the Prophet, for the Muhammadans who accompanied him in his army in the expedition against Baghdad had warned him that if the blood of the Khalīfah was shed upon the ground the world would be overspread with darkness and the army of the Mongols be swallowed up by an earthquake.

It is difficult to estimate the bewilderment that

* Even as early as the eighth century, superstition had regarded the Caliphs as free from the attacks of plague.[6]

Muslims felt when there was no longer a Caliph on whom the blessing of God could be invoked in the Khuṭbah; such an event was without precedent throughout the previous history of Islam. Their suffering finds expression in the prayer offered in the great mosque of Baghdad on the Friday following the death of the Caliph: 'Praise be to God who has caused exalted personages to perish and has given over to destruction the inhabitants of this city. . . . O God, help us in our misery, the like of which Islam and its children have never witnessed; we are God's and unto God do we return.' [7]

When pious souls in later years looked back upon this tragedy in Baghdad, they realized how its horror had been prognosticated by terrible portents, e. g. a furious rushing wind had torn the curtain from the Ka'bah so that it remained bare for twenty-one days; an earthquake had shaken the Minbar of the Prophet in the mosque of Medina; fire had burst forth from a hill at Aden, and numerous other prophetic horrors, fire, flood, and plague, had marked the approach of this dread disaster that caused the Muslim world to be without a Khalīfah for three years and a half.[8]

But so long as there was a Caliph in Baghdad various Muslim princes, either for political reasons or out of pious feeling, acknowledged his nominal headship of the Muhammadan world. Such a recognition as was given by the powerful monarch in the East, Maḥmūd of Ghazna, at the close of the tenth century, came nearly a century later from the distant West, when about 1086 Yūsuf ibn Tāshfīn, who was destined to establish the Almoravid dynasty in Spain, sent a request to the Caliph Muqtadī that he would confirm him in the possession of his dominions. The Caliph replied by sending him robes of honour and standards, and bestowing upon him the new title of Amīr ul-Muslimīn. This is startingly like the Caliph's own title of Amīr ul-Mu'minīn, and probably the Caliph merely gave his consent to the use of a title which Yūsuf ibn Tāshfīn had already himself assumed. If the Caliph had wished to protest, he was in much too weak a position to make any such protest effective, and he was probably only too pleased to receive this recognition of his theoretical overlordship in the world of Islam, a recognition that was so markedly in contrast to his dependent position under the Saljūq. Moreover, such a submission was all the more impressive as coming from Spain, which, for a century and a half had upheld an independent Caliphate of its own. Yūsuf ibn Tāshfīn, while arrogating to himself none of the actual titles of the Caliph, probably invented as a mark of his own dignity this title of Amīr ul-Muslimīn as setting him up above all other Sunnī princes by its very obvious resemblance to the designation of every Caliph since the great days of 'Umar.

The Almoravid movement began as an orthodox propaganda among the Berbers in North Africa, and stirred up this vigorous race to a career of conquest, of which the foundation of Morocco is a permanent memorial. But in less than a century their power had declined, for they failed to fulfil the promise of their brilliant successes when they had crossed over into Spain and defeated the Christian forces in the battle of Zallaka (1086), and a few years later added the provinces of Muhammadan Spain to their empire. Their dynasty was swept away in 1146 by the new movement of the Almohads, who also arose among the Berbers, and, as will be shown later, claimed to have an Imām of their own. But the recognition of the Abbasid Caliph by the Almoravids, so long as this dynasty lasted, constituted a distinct addition to his prestige; and there was some compensation for the disappearance of the Almoravids, when, in 1171, the news reached Baghdad that the rival Fatimid Caliphate in Cairo had come to an end. For more than two centuries and a half the Shiah Caliph had flaunted the claim of the Abbasids to the headship of Islam and had enjoyed immense wealth and power in the possession of Egypt and Syria, while the Abbasids in Baghdad had been suffering a miserable decline. A new champion of Islam had appeared, and the victorious career of Saladin had raised up new hopes in the Muslim world. He signalized his conquest of Egypt, as soon as he felt his position secure in that country, by displacing the Shiah Caliph, whose wazīr he was supposed to be, and the faithful once more prayed for the Abbasid Caliph in the mosques of Cairo and the other cities of Egypt. Muqtadī had the city of Baghdad illuminated in honour of this great event, and sent flags and robes of honour to Saladin, the champion of orthodoxy.

A few years later, in 1174, Saladin displaced the youthful heir of his deceased master, Nūr ud-Dīn, who had died in May of that year, and himself assumed the royal title. In 1175 he wrote to the Caliph, Mustaḍī, announcing his victory over the Franks and his conquests in the Yaman and in North Africa, and reminded the Caliph how he had established the Khuṭbah in Egypt in the name of the Abbasid, and asked for a diploma of investiture over Egypt, the Maghrib, the Yaman, and Syria; the Caliph gave away what was not his to give, but what it was flattering to him not to refuse, and sent the required diploma together with a robe of honour.

The founder of another dynasty—this time in the south, in the Yaman—Nūr ud-Dīn 'Umar (1229–1249), the Rasūlid, in 1234, sent large presents to the Caliph Mustanṣir, asking for the title of Sulṭān and a diploma of investiture as his lieutenant. The Caliph was naturally delighted to receive such a recognition of his office, but it was characteristic of the lack of real authority in his hands that his envoys carrying the diploma were unable to make their way by land to the Yaman; they joined the pilgrim-caravan that had set out from 'Iraq to Mecca, but the Arabs blocked their way, and all the pilgrims had to return to Baghdad. It was not until the following year that it was possible to send the diploma by sea; whereupon the envoy of the Khalīfah ascending the pulpit delivered the message of his master, conferring on Nūr ud-Dīn 'Umar the governorship of the Yaman, and clothed him with a robe of honour.[9]

Still more interesting is the homage that came, for the first time, from India. Here the Muslim conquests had resulted in the submission of nearly the whole of Northern India, and a dynasty had been established, known as that of the 'Slave Kings', because the first monarchs of this dynasty had been Turkish slaves, who, distinguishing themselves by their military prowess, had been appointed generals of armies and afterwards governors of provinces. One of these, named Iltutmish, in 1211 set aside the son of his predecessor and brought the greater part of Hindustan under his subjection. Iltutmish apparently felt the need of some legal sanction for his usurpation. But he had already been for some years on the throne of Delhi before he made his application to the Caliph, and it was not until 1229 that a diploma of investiture was sent by Mustanṣir, confirming Iltutmish in the possession of all the lands and seas he had conquered and bestowing upon him the title of the great Sultan. The document was solemnly read out in a vast assembly held in Delhi, and Iltutmish from that date put the name of the Caliph on his coins.

His successors followed this pious example. The name of the last Abbasid Khalīfah of Baghdad, Musta'ṣim (1242–1258), first appears on the coins of 'Alā ud-Dīn Mas'ūd Shāh (1241–1246); and though Musta'ṣim was put to death by the Mongols in 1258, his name still appears on the coins of successive kings of Delhi, e.g. Maḥmūd Shāh Nāṣir ud-Dīn (1246–1265), Ghiyāth ud-Dīn Balban (1265–1287), and Mu'izz ud-Dīn Kayqubād (1287–1290), the last monarch of the so-called 'Slave' dynasty; and the first of these continued to have the name of Musta'ṣim mentioned in the Khuṭbah.[10]

A new dynasty arose, that of the Khaljī; the same need for legitimization was apparently still felt, and the coins of Jalāl ud-Dīn Fīrūz Shāh II (1290–1295) continued to bear the name of Musta'ṣim, though this Caliph had been trampled to death by the Mongols more than thirty years before.[11]

What was an unfortunate Muslim monarch to do, who felt that his title was insecure? He knew that it was only his sword that had set him on the throne, that his own dynasty might at any time be displaced, as he had himself displaced the dynasty that had preceded him, while his legal advisers and religious guides told him that the only legitimate source of authority was the Khalīfah, the Imām, and he realized that all his devout Muslim subjects shared their opinion. So he went on putting the name of the dead Musta'ṣim on his coins, because he could find no other, and the Muslim theory of the state had not succeeded in adjusting itself to the fact that there was no Khalīfah or Imām in existence. His successor, 'Alā ud-Dīn Muḥammad Shāh I (1295–1315), got out of the difficulty by ceasing to insert Musta'ṣim's name and by describing himself merely as Yamīn ul-Khilāfat Nāṣir Amīri 'l-Mu'minīn, 'The right hand of the Caliphate, the helper of the Commander of the Faithful',[12] and this was sufficient for the satisfaction of tender consciences, though in reality he was giving no help at all to any Caliph, any more than either of his predecessors had done who had seen the unhappy Musta'ṣim trampled to death without moving a finger, though they had gone on making use of his name, for their own selfish political purposes.

The situation was no doubt a puzzling one, even as it was unprecedented. The Muslim world found by experience that it had to get on without a Caliph and this circumstance undoubtedly made an impression on the minds of thinking men. It is probable that from this period the opinion gained strength that the institution of the Caliphate had really ceased in the apostolic age. This was a doctrine that had found expression much earlier, and (as will be seen later on) has been from time to time revived.

VII

ESTABLISHMENT OF THE ABBASID CALIPHATE IN CAIRO

Though the Caliphate had in this tragic manner ceased to exist, politicians could not forget the important part that the Caliph had played in the political life of the Muhammadan world, by giving a show of legitimacy to such monarchs as had by murder or usurpation, or by their military prowess, established themselves upon a throne and afterwards sought for a title to it.

Such a difficulty arose in Egypt in the period of the decay of the Ayyūbid dynasty that had been founded by Saladin, when fifty years after this great monarch's death the reins of power were slipping from the weak hands of his successors, and the administration of the country had passed to Mamlūk Amīrs—Turkish slaves, who had risen to commanding positions in the army. These Mamlūks who, for more than two centuries and a half, ruled the rich lands of Egypt, first endeavoured to give an appearance of legitimacy to their rule by pretending to govern the country as viceroys for infant princes, e.g. Aybak (1250–1257), for a child of the Ayyūbid family and a descendant of Saladin, and Aybak's successor, Qutuz (1257–1259), for the infant child of Aybak; but this was an unsatisfactory arrangement, and both of these Mamlūk Amīrs found it necessary after a short time to thrust aside the nominal Sultan and assume sovereignty in their own name. The fourth Mamlūk ruler, Baybars (1260–1277), extricated himself from this difficult situation by inviting an uncle of the last Abbasid Caliph, who had managed to escape the massacre in Baghdad, to come to Cairo. He was escorted into the city with great pomp and ceremony in June 1261 and was there installed as Caliph. After his genealogy had been investigated by the jurists, the chief Qāḍī solemnly attested its correctness and took the oath of allegiance to him, followed by Baybars and the officers of state, promising to obey the ordinances of the Word of God and of the Traditions, and to fight in defence of the faith. A few days later the Caliph, who assumed the title of Mustanṣir, by which his brother, the penultimate Caliph (1226–1242) had been known, with due solemnity conferred upon Baybars a robe of honour together with a diploma of investiture, which was couched in the following terms: 'Praise be to God who has displayed upon Islam the robes of glory, and has made the brightness of its pearls shine forth, that aforetime were hidden under a thick shell; and has so firmly established the edifice of its prosperity that thereby He has caused all record of what went before to be forgotten; and has ordained for its support kings with whom even those who otherwise differ are in agreement. . . . I bear witness that there is no God save God, One, without a partner. . . . I bear witness that our

Lord Muḥammad is His servant and His Apostle, who has repaired the breaches of the faith and has displayed all manner of noble qualities (may God bless him and his family, the memorial of whose virtues will never perish, and his Companions who wrought noble deeds in the faith and merited increase in good things !). Now, that ruler is most deserving of honour and good report and most worthy that the pen should bow down and prostrate itself while writing the recital of his virtues and his righteous deeds, who puts forth all his efforts and sees praise coming to meet them, who calls on men to obey him . . . and ever sets his hand to generous deeds with might and main, and, sword in hand, never destroys the hiding-place of error, without giving it over to the flames and drenching it in blood. Since all these noble qualities are the special characteristics of his sublime highness, Sultan Malik uẓ-Ẓāhir Rukn ud-Dīn (may God ennoble and exalt him !), the High Chancellery of the descendant of the Prophet, the Imām Mustanṣir (may God exalt his power), has been pleased to extol the lofty merit of this prince and to proclaim his good offices, which even the most eloquent language would fail adequately to express or fittingly commend, for it is he who has raised up again the Abbasid dynasty after it had been crippled by the blows of ill-fortune and robbed of all its welfare and blessings ; on its behalf he has reproved its adverse fortune and has won for it the favour and goodwill of fate, that had attacked it with destructive fury; he has taken captive the ill-fortune that was once its bitter enemy; he has lavished his care upon it and has turned away from it all its woes. He showed kindness and sympathy to the Commander of the Faithful as soon as he arrived, and displayed conspicuous eagerness for divine reward, and exhibited such zeal for the cause of the holy law and for the paying of homage by the nobles, that if any other had set his hand to this task, he must inevitably have failed. But God has bestowed upon him such abundant virtue, in order that the scale of his merits may be weighted down thereby and the account that he will have to render on the Day of Judgement may be lightened. . . . Therefore the Commander of the Faithful gives you thanks for such kindness, and makes known to all, that but for your watchful care, the ruin would have been without repair. He confers on you authority over Egypt, Syria, Diyar Bakr, the Hijaz, the Yaman, the land of the Euphrates and whatever fresh conquests you may achieve, on plain or mountain. He entrusts to you the government of them and the control of their troops and their population, so that you may become for them a paragon of generosity, and he makes no exception of any single city or fortress or any object, great or small. Then keep a watch over the interests of the whole body of the faithful, since this burden has been laid upon you.' Then follow exhortations to righteous government, and a number of directions as to the appointment and supervision of officials, the abolition of oppressive taxation, &c. The Caliph next emphasizes his own claim to recognition in an impressive and emphatic manner, with the words, 'I offer praise to God for that He has set by your side an Imām to guide you in the right way; it is your bounden duty to show him the greatest possible honour.' Lastly, he urges the Sultan to prosecute with zeal the war against unbelievers, saying, 'One of the matters of which mention must be made is the divine command to wage Jihād, for this is an obligation resting upon the whole body of the faithful, and an achievement that shines out brightly on the pages of history. God has promised a rich reward to those who fight in Jihād, and has reserved for them a high place near Himself, and has assigned to them a special seat in Paradise, wherein is no vain discourse or incitement to sin. . . . Through you God has preserved the defences of Islām from desecration, and by your firm resolution has maintained for the Muslims good order in these realms, and your sword has inflicted incurable wounds on the hearts of the unbelievers. Through you we hope that the Caliphate will regain its ancient glory. Then for the sake of the victory of Islām be watchful and let not your eyes be heedless or asleep. In waging Jihād against the enemies of God, be a leader that is followed and follows none, and support the doctrine of the Unity of God, and you will find all men ready to follow and obey you in support of it.' Then come various instructions as to the protection of the frontiers, the repair of fortified places, and the equipment of the fleet. At the conclusion of the ceremony, the Sultan made a triumphal progress through the city of Cairo, accompanied by his officers of state, one of whom bore the diploma of investiture in front of him.[1]

One of the most remarkable features of this document is the assumption of authority by the Caliph over territories that had not owed allegiance to the Abbasid dynasty for centuries, his claim to supreme jurisdiction in the Muslim world, though he himself had no troops or resources of any kind at his disposal, and his interference, though an entire stranger, in the administrative details of so highly organized a bureaucratic system as that of the government of Egypt. Baybars might well have felt doubts as to the wisdom of the action he had taken in welcoming the Abbasid prince into his capital, and he seems to have at once set about making preparations for the departure of his guest, who was to be provided with troops for the reconquest of Baghdad. About three months later they set out together from Cairo, with a large force, but when they reached Damascus, Baybars was warned by a friend that the re-establishment of the Caliphate in Baghdad might endanger his own independence; so he abandoned the unfortunate Mustanṣir to his fate, and the Caliph, while making his way across the desert with a small body of troops, was attacked by the Mongol governor of Baghdad, and nothing more was ever heard of him.

A year later another prince of the Abbasid family, Abu'l 'Abbās Aḥmad, who escaped the disaster that befell Mustanṣir, made his way to Cairo, and after some delay was there installed as Khalīfah with the title of Ḥākim; but this time Baybars took care not to have a rival to his own power, and though he treated the Caliph with every mark of outward respect, he practically kept him a prisoner in the citadel and allowed him to exercise no influence in the political life of the country.

The same forms and ceremonies were observed as in the case of Mustanṣir; the genealogy of the fugitive was scrutinized and declared to be authentic by the chief Qāḍī, but Baybars allowed nearly a year to elapse, during which coins continued to be struck in the name of Mustanṣir, before arranging in November 1262 for the formal ceremony of paying allegiance to the new Caliph, who in return conferred upon him royal authority. The next day was Friday and the Caliph delivered the following Khuṭbah: 'Praise be to God who has raised up for the family of 'Abbās a pillar and a helper, and has appointed for them a Sultan as their defender. I praise Him both for good and evil days; may He help me to give thanks for the blessings He has lavished upon me, and make me victorious over my enemies. I bear witness that there is no God save God, One only, without a partner, and that Muḥammad is His servant and His Apostle (may God bless him, his family and his Companions, those stars to guide men aright, those Imāms who are patterns of righteousness, the four first Caliphs, and 'Abbās, his paternal uncle, the consoler of his griefs, and the illustrious, rightly-guided Caliphs, and the Imāms who followed on the right way, and the other Companions and those who followed after them! May God pour His blessings upon them until the Day of Judgement!). Know, O ye men, that the Imāmate is one of the obligations of Islam, and that Jihād is binding on all men; that the standard of Jihād cannot be upraised unless men are united; that women can only be led away into captivity when the obligations of honour are violated; that blood can only be shed through sin and wickedness. You have seen the enemies of Islam enter the Abode of Peace (i. e. Baghdad), sacrificing blood and riches, slaying men and children, profaning the sanctuary and the sacred precincts of the Khilāfat, and inflicting upon those they left alive the most terrible sufferings; everywhere there rose up cries of lamentation and wailing; everywhere were heard cries of terror by reason of the horrors of this long drawn out day. How many old men had their white hair stained with blood! How many children wept and there was none to take pity on their tears! Then gird up your loins in your efforts to fulfil the obligation of Jihād. Fear God while ye are able. Hear and obey, spend the wealth of your own lives. Those who refrain from being niggardly of their lives will assuredly be blessed. There is no longer any excuse to prevent you from attacking the enemies of religion and from defending the Muslims. This Sultan Malik uẓ-Ẓāhir, the illustrious, wise and just ruler, who wages Jihād and brings succour, the pillar of the world and of religion, has risen up to defend the Imāmate, when there were but few to help it, and he has scattered the armies of the unbelievers when they had already begun to pry into the recesses of our dwellings. Through his care the oath of allegiance has been taken by men who have bound themselves by covenant, and the Abbasid dynasty has thereby gained numerous soldiers. Servants of God, make haste to show your gratitude for such a blessing; purify your intentions and you will be victorious; fight against the followers of the Devil and you will gain the advantage; do not let yourselves be terrified by past events, for war has its chances, but success in the end comes to the God-fearing. Time endures but for two days, and the next world is reserved for the true believers. May God unite you all on the basis of piety and give you a glorious victory through the faith. Pray God to pardon me, yourselves and all Muslims; pray for His forgiveness, for He is forgiving and compassionate.' The Caliph then sat down for a while in accordance with the usual custom, and rising up again began the second part of the Khuṭbah, consisting merely of pious ejaculations and prayers for the blessing of God.[2]

Such was the beginning of a long line of Caliphs in Cairo, one descendant of Ḥākim after another occupying this office for two centuries and a half. They were even more powerless and ineffectual than the later Abbasids in Baghdad had been ; but their presence in Cairo gave a show of legitimacy to Mamlūk rule in Egypt, and the Caliph used to be brought out from his seclusion on the occasion of the accession of each new Sultan, in order to invest him with authority and give to his rule the sanction of the law.

How much importance Sultan Baybars attached to his having secured in his capital the presence of the Caliph, though he kept him as a virtual prisoner, may be judged from the fact that, on a tablet at Homs commemorating the endowments he had bestowed on the grave of Khālid ibn al-Walīd, the conqueror of Syria, he sums up a long string of titles with the statement that it was he ‘ who had given orders for allegiance to be paid to the two Khalīfahs ’.[3]

VIII

RELATIONS OF THE ABBASID CALIPHS IN CAIRO WITH OTHER PRINCES IN THE MUSLIM WORLD

For more than two centuries and a half, thirteen other members of the same family held the shadowy office of Khalīfah in Cairo. They were brought out with great pomp and ceremony to instal each successive Mamlūk Sultan who rose to power, often after the assassination of his predecessor, and (as will be seen) other Muslim princes made use of them to give a show of legitimacy to their rule. But the presence in Cairo of the theoretical source of all authority in the Muslim world made the Mamlūk ruler claim for himself a higher status than that of any other Muhammadan ruler and deny to any of his rivals the right to assume the title of Sultan, for on him alone was it conferred by the Caliph in accordance with the prescriptions of the Holy Law.[1]

The position of the Abbasid Caliphs in Cairo was a very humiliating one, and contemporary historians have not hesitated to speak freely about their dependent condition. One of the greatest of the Mamlūk Sultans, Qalā'ūn (1279–1290), never even condescended to ask the Caliph to invest him with authority. A later Sultan—about the middle of the fourteenth century—Nāṣir Muḥammad, deprived the Caliph, Wāthiq bi'llāhi

Ibrāhīm, for some months even of the empty dignity of having his name mentioned in the Khuṭbah, and as the Muslim historian laments, 'The name of the Caliph passed from the pulpits as if it had never risen above them, and the prayer for the Caliphs vacated the mihrabs of the mosque as if it had never reverberated at their gate.'[2] Moreover, the allowance granted to this Caliph was so scanty that the populace in derision nicknamed him 'the beggar'.[3]

But whatever might be the practice in Egypt, to none of these Abbasid Caliphs (with the single exception to be mentioned later) was the privilege accorded of having his name mentioned in the Khuṭbah in the Holy City of Mecca. Since the murder of the last Abbasid Caliph of Baghdad, Musta'ṣim, in 1258, no Caliph had been prayed for in the great Friday services round the Ka'bah, the centre of Islamic unity, either because the ecclesiastical authorities concerned believed that the Muslim world was now without a Khalīfah, or else (in view of the fact that there were other claimants) from a special distrust of the claim made by the Caliphs in Cairo to the possession of that dignity. The reason they alleged was that none of these fainéant Caliphs struck coins in his own name or issued decrees from a chancellery of his own; they obviously held the theory that the office of the Caliphate implied *de facto* sovereignty.[4] The one exception was when the Caliph Musta'īn was made the plaything of rival political factions and was elected Sultan of Egypt in 1412, only to find that he was as much a prisoner as before and that all actual power was in the hands of others; six months later he was compelled to resign his office into the hands of the man whose tool he had been, who now had himself proclaimed Sultan as al-Malik al-Mu'ayyad.[5]

Another historian, Suyūṭī, writing at the end of the fifteenth century, also speaks of the subordinate position that the Caliph occupied in his day; he writes: 'Things have come to such a pass in our time that the Caliph visits the Sultan to congratulate him at the beginning of every month, and the utmost that the Sultan condescends in his favour is to come down from his dais and the two sit down together beyond the dais; then the Caliph gets up and goes away like an ordinary person and the Sultan seats himself again upon his throne of state.'[6]

Still the theorists could look upon the Caliph in Cairo as ruler over all Muslim territories and as head of the Muslim community. Khalīl ibn Shāhīn aẓ-Ẓāhirī (1410–1468), who wrote a book on the organization of the Mamlūk state, describes the Amīr ul-Mu'minīn as follows: 'He is the Khalīfah of God on His earth, cousin of His apostle, the chief of the apostles, and has inherited the Khilāfat from him (the Prophet). God Almighty has made him (the Khalīfah) ruler over the whole land of Islam. None of the kings of the East or the West can hold the title of Sultan, unless there be a covenant between him and the

Khalīfah. Some religious authorities have laid it down that any one who sets himself up as a Sultan by violence, by means of the sword, and without a compact with the Khalīfah, is a rebel and cannot appoint any one as an official or qāḍī; if any one is so appointed, the decisions and marriage contracts they make are invalid.' [7]

In the fifteenth century we have a description of the Caliph accompanying the Mamlūk Sultan, Barsbay (1422–1438), on a campaign, as riding before him and acting as his chamberlain, while all dignity and honour were reserved for the Sultan, the Caliph appearing merely as one of the nobles in the Sultan's suite.[8]

Maqrīzī, who died in 1441, makes the following contemptuous remarks upon this institution: 'The Mamlūks installed as Caliph a man to whom they gave this name and the titles that went with it, but he had no remnant of authority, not even the right of expressing his opinion. He spent his time among the nobles, the high officials, scribes, and judges, paying them visits to thank them for the dinners and entertainments to which they had invited him.' [9]

In spite of such conditions of humiliation, there were other Muslim princes besides the Mamlūks, who found the Abbasid Caliph in Cairo useful, as giving a title to the possession of dominions acquired by fraud or force. The founder of the Muzaffarid dynasty, which ruled in southern Persia for eighty years (1313–1393), Mubāriz ud-Dīn Muḥammad ibn Muẓaffar, threw off his allegiance to his overlord, the Mongol Īlkhān, and started on a career of conquest. Towards the end of his career—(he was deposed and blinded in 1357)—he took the oath of allegiance to the Caliph, Mu'taḍid bi'llāhi, in 1354, and after his capture of Tabriz in 1357, had the Caliph's name inserted in the Khuṭbah. His son, Shāh Shujā' (1357–1384), similarly recognized the Caliph, Mutawakkil, in 1369.[10]

There are circumstances of special interest connected with the recognition of the fainéant Caliph of Cairo by the Turkish Sultans of Delhi. In 1325 Muḥammad ibn Tughlaq came to the throne by murdering his father under circumstances of peculiar treachery. He had had a temporary wooden structure erected for his father's accommodation, and arranged that during a parade of the state elephants, they should collide with the building, so that it buried in its fall the Sultan and his favourite son, while Muḥammad took care that assistance should be delayed until it was too late. The new monarch was one of the most remarkable figures in the history of Muhammadan India. His oppressive government ruined the country and drove his subjects into rebellion; whereupon he massacred them without mercy; even in normal times he appears to have had a lust for blood and a passion for savage executions. He indulged in wild schemes of administration and conquest that resulted in widespread misery; one of his mad ideas was to change the capital from

Delhi to Daulatābād, a distance of forty days' journey; accordingly the whole population of this vast city was turned out of their homes, and many of them perished on the journey. The Sultan's officers made a rigorous search for any who had evaded his orders and remained behind; they found two men in the city, one a paralytic and the other blind; these men were brought before the Sultan, who ordered the paralytic to be shot from a catapult, and the blind man to be dragged from Delhi to Daulatābād; he fell to pieces during the journey and only one of his legs reached the new capital. But Muḥammad ibn Tughlaq was a pious Muslim, regular in his devotions, abstaining from wine, and scrupulous in the observance of the precepts of his faith. He had been on the throne for upwards of eighteen years when he began to be troubled with doubts as to the legitimacy of his rule, inasmuch as it had not received the confirmation of the Abbasid Caliph. So he made inquiries from a great many travellers and discovered that there was an Abbasid Caliph named Mustakfī, in Egypt. He entered into correspondence with him, and when a diploma of investiture was sent from Cairo, Sultan Muḥammad received it with marks of exaggerated respect, had the Caliph's name inserted in the Khuṭbah and struck upon his coins, and sent rich presents to the Caliph in return.[11] How little in the matter of personal relations was implied by this exchange of compliments may be judged from the fact that the name of Mustakfī, who died in 1340, continued to appear on the coins of Muḥammad ibn Tughlaq up to the years 1342 and 1343, with the prayer 'May God make his Caliphate abide for ever'.[12]

His pious successor, Fīrūz Shāh (1351–1388), who was as gentle as Muḥammad ibn Tughlaq had been savage, made a similar submission to the Caliph in Cairo, and in an interesting little autobiographical sketch which he wrote, he thus makes reference to his attitude of mind in the matter:

'The greatest and best of honours that I obtained through God's mercy was, that by my obedience and piety, and friendliness and submission to the Khalīfah, the representative of the holy Prophet, my authority was confirmed; for it is by his sanction that the power of kings is assured, and no king is secure until he has submitted himself to the Khalīfah and has received a confirmation from the sacred throne. A diploma was sent to me fully confirming my authority as deputy of the Khilāfat, and the leader of the faithful was graciously pleased to honour me with the title of Sayyid us-Salāṭīn. He also bestowed upon me robes, a banner, a sword, a ring, and a foot-print as badges of honour and distinction.'[13]

In Transoxiana also it was felt that the Abbasid Caliph in Cairo might be madé use of for dynastic purposes. Tīmūr had nominated his grandson, Pīr Muḥammad, as his heir, but when the conqueror died in 1404 there was at once a scramble for the possession of his vast empire, and Pīr

Muḥammad found his claim opposed by his cousin, Khalīl Sulṭān. Some of his supporters urged him to apply for a royal diploma from the Abbasid Caliphs in Cairo, and thus annul the laws accepted by the Mongols (i. e. the Yāsāq). It was a poor expedient at the best, but it was an expression of belief in the power of an appeal to Muhammadan sentiment, by recognition of the lost ideals of the Muslim world, the supremacy of the Caliph and the authority of the Sharī'ah.[14] But the proposal does not appear to have been adopted; Pīr Muḥammad decided to recognize the overlordship of his uncle, Shāh Rukh, and was murdered two years after his grandfather's death.

It was probably a similar desire to find political support that led the Ottoman Sultan Bāyazīd I, in 1394, to apply to the Abbasid Caliph in Cairo for the formal grant of the title of Sultan.[15] There is no evidence that this request for formal recognition was ever granted, and doubt has been thrown on the possibility of its ever having been made,[16] but in a letter that Bāyazīd wrote about 1400 to Tīmūr, he reminded him of the Abbasids, 'heirs of the throne of the Caliphate', who had taken refuge in Egypt[17]—as if to give the ruthless conqueror a hint that there was still a possible centre of common Muslim effort, or that at least Turks and Egyptians could be joined together by the memory of a once undivided Muslim empire, to resist the destruction that Tīmūr was working among the faithful.

IX

ASSUMPTION OF THE TITLE KHALĪFAH BY INDEPENDENT MUSLIM PRINCES

WHILE some Muslim potentates believed that there was still a Khalīfah in existence as head of the Muslim world, there were others who mocked at the pretensions of the Abbasid Caliphs of Cairo. There were some persons who cast doubt upon their genealogy and did not accept their claim to be descended from the Caliphs of Baghdad; others revived the theory, to which reference has already been made, that the Caliphate had really lasted for only thirty years. This doctrine had found expression in the authoritative collections of Traditions, and accordingly must have come into existence so early as the third century of the Muhammadan era, e.g. one Tradition represents the Prophet as saying: 'The Caliphate after me will endure for thirty years; then will come the rule of a king.'[1] The historian, Maqrīzī, to whom reference has already been made several times, adopts this doctrine when he says that after the four rightly directed Caliphs, that is, after the death of 'Alī (661), with the rise of the Umayyads the Caliphate had became a kingdom characterized by violence and tyranny. The great jurist, Ibn Khaldūn, held that after the reign of Hārūn ur-Rashīd, there was left of the Caliphate nothing but the name, since by that time it had become transformed into a mere kingdom, and that with the disappearance of the hegemony of the Arab race the office of the Khalīfah had ceased to exist.[2] A later writer, Quṭb ud-Dīn, who died in 1582, speaks quite as emphatically, but dates the disappearance of the Caliphate from the death of the last Caliph of Baghdad at the hands of the Mongols in 1258 ; [3] he reiterates the opinion that the Caliphs of Cairo were Caliphs only in name and that there was no meaning whatsoever in their being so styled.[4]

Such thinkers clearly recognized that there was a disparity between the subservient position of the Caliph and the pretentious claims associated with his title, e. g. that he was the protector of Islam and should wage war against its enemies, &c. There was doubtless a growing feeling that political power and the control of armed force should be conjoined with such high pretensions. As early as the period when the Buwayhids were holding the Abbasid Caliph of Baghdad in tutelage, a distinguished Sunnī theologian, al-Bāqilānī, who died in that city in 1012 during the reign of the insignificant Qādir, had declared that the Caliph need not be of the Quraysh, seeing that this tribe had by that time become so degenerate and feeble.[5]

When the doctors of the law could so boldly express themselves and cast doubt upon the claim of the Abbasid Caliph in Cairo to represent the headship of the Muslim world, it was but natural that the men of the sword, who had carved out for themselves kingdoms and taken advantage of the disturbed state of society to set themselves up as independent sovereigns, should not have hesitated to make the boldest assertions of their own dignity. This is especially characteristic of the Mongols into whose hands the greater part of the eastern provinces of the original Arab empire had passed. Though the Mongol princes of Persia and other countries ultimately adopted Islam, they still remained for some time under the influence of the ancient Mongol constitution, the so-called Yāsāq, the code of regulations embodying the primitive Turkish and Mongol customs.[6]

When one of these Mongol princes came entirely under the influence of the Muslim 'Ulamā, he would substitute for this tribal system of law the Sharī'ah, but such a process was slow in view of the impressive character of the Mongol conquests. The masterful descendants of Chingīz Khān were more ready to put forward descent from this world-conqueror as a justification for their exercise of authority than seek a diploma of investiture from the alleged descendants of that Abbasid Caliph whom their relatives had put to death in 1258. The vastness of the Mongol empire with its admirable administration, that made it possible for travellers to pass with safety from China to the eastern frontiers of the Byzantine empire, constituted a more impressive spectacle in the political world than was afforded by the story of the powerless and ineffectual Caliphs during the latter days of the Abbasids in Baghdad, to say nothing of the fainéant Caliphs in Cairo.

Accordingly we find that even such a zealous Muslim as Ghāzān Khān, the Īlkhān of Persia (1295–1304), who had made Islam the state religion throughout his dominions and built many mosques and endowed colleges, could boast of his descent from the pitiless Mongol conqueror who had put to death countless Musalmans and had devastated the great centres of Muslim civilization in Central Asia. Ghāzān Khān was the great grandson of Hūlāgū, the conqueror of Baghdad, and had been brought up as a Buddhist, but had been converted to Islam before he came to the throne in 1295. He avenged the check inflicted by the Egyptians on the armies of his ancestor Hūlāgū in the battle of 'Ayn Jālūt (1260), by attacking Syria and occupying Damascus in December 1299, after inflicting a crushing defeat on the Egyptian army. When he received a deputation from the leading men of the city, he asked them 'Who am I'? With one accord they replied 'Shāh Ghāzān, son of Arghūn Khān, son of Abāqā Khān, son of Hūlāgū Khān, son of Tulūy Khān, son of Chinghīz Khān'. Then he asked, 'Who was the father of Nāṣir?' (the Mamlūk Sultan); and though they could give the name of his father, no one knew the name of the boy-king's grandfather (he was only fourteen at the time). So the deputation was put to silence, recognizing that no rightful claim could be made out for the Mamlūk prince, and prayed to God for blessings on 'the Pādshāh of Islam'.[7] Thus Ghāzān Khān felt that he needed no authorization from the Abbasid in Cairo, nor would his dignity be enhanced by the assumption of the title of Caliph; accordingly after his occupation of Damascus he was described in the Khuṭbah merely as 'the august Sultan, the Sultan of Islam and the Muslims'.[8]

But as the Mongols became more completely Islamized and the Muslim law, the Sharī'ah, displaced the heathen Yāsāq, pious Muslim monarchs naturally ceased to boast of their descent from Chingīz Khān or other enemies of the faith; but then on the other hand, they did not turn to the insignificant Abbasid Caliph in Cairo for ratification of their claim on the obedience of their subjects. It became customary to appeal directly to God Himself. When Khalīl Sulṭān, a grandson of Tīmūr, was asked by what right he had set himself up in Samarqand as successor to the empire of his grandfather—had Tīmūr bequeathed to him the throne and the kingdom in his will?—he replied: 'The Almighty who gave the throne and the kingdom to Tīmūr, has bestowed it also upon me.'[9] He was soon thrust aside by his abler and more energetic uncle, Shāh Rukh, who appealed to the same irrefragable source of authority, declaring: 'God alone is immortal; to Him alone belongs dominion; He giveth and taketh it away as it pleaseth Him.' The theologians found justification in the Word of God for this direct appeal to divine appointment, by quoting from the Qur'ān the verse; 'O God, king of the kingdom, Thou givest the kingdom to whomsoever Thou wilt, and Thou takest away the kingdom from whomsoever Thou wilt, and Thou raisest to honour whomsoever Thou wilt, and Thou abasest whomsoever Thou wilt' (iii. 25). In accordance with this high claim of divine appointment and his exalted position in the Muhammadan world, Shāh Rukh undoubtedly cherished the ambition of being recognized as Khalīfah and overlord of other Muslim princes. That his near neighbours who had reason to dread his armies should acquiesce in his pretentious claim, is not surprising, and Qara Yūsuf, chief of the Turkomans of the Black Sheep dynasty, writing about 1416 to the Ottoman Sultan, Muḥammad I, to warn him of the aggressive policy of the Timurid monarch, speaks of him as 'Shāh Rukh Bahādur Gūrgānī, may God make the days of his Caliphate endure for ever',[10] and Hamzah Beg, chief of the Turkomans of the White Sheep from 1406 to 1444, refers to him as 'the shadow of God upon earth', in a letter to Sultan Murād II.[11] Even Muḥammad I found it politic in writing to Shāh Rukh in 1416, to address him as 'Your exalted majesty, who has attained the pre-eminent rank of the Caliphate'.[12]

But it was another matter when he attempted to impose his authority on independent princes whose geographical position put them at a safer distance from his aggression. In January 1436 Barsbay, the Mamlūk Sultan of Egypt, received an embassy from Shāh Rukh, demanding that he should recognize him as his overlord, apply to him for a patent of investiture, strike coins in his name, and have mention made of him in the Khuṭbah. Barsbay tore in pieces the robe of honour that Shāh Rukh had sent, had his envoy cudgelled and thrown into a tank, so that he was in danger of being drowned and nearly died of cold, and sent back a message that he dared Shāh Rukh to come in person to Egypt, to avenge the insults paid to his ambassador. At the same time Barsbay wrote to Sultan Murād II, who had received a similar invitation but had treated the matter as a jest, and invited him to join him in an alliance against Shāh Rukh.[13] Equally unsuccessful were Shāh Rukh's efforts in India; the unfortunate 'Abd ur-Razzāq has left us a vivid account of the miserable failure of his embassy to the Zamorin of Calicut;[14] and if it is true that the insignificant Khiẓr Khān of the so-called Sayyid dynasty in Delhi (1414–1421) caused the Khuṭbah to be read in the name of Shāh Rukh, as he had done for his father, Tīmūr, before him,[15] then this was an achievement hardly worth boasting of, since Khiẓr Khān's authority was confined within a very limited area and indeed barely extended outside the city of Delhi. Shāh Rukh himself provided the text of the Khuṭbah that Khiẓr Khān was to have read: 'O God, cause the foundations of the kingdom and of the religion to abide for ever, uplift the banner of Islam, and strengthen the pillars of the incontestible Sharī'at, by maintaining the kingdom of the exalted Sulṭān, the just Khāqān, the noble overlord of the necks of the nations, the ruler of the sultans of the Arabs and non-Arabs, the shadow of God upon earth, the ruler over land and sea, who enlarges the foundations of peace and security, who uplifts the banner of justice and benevolence, who protects the territories of God, who gives help to the servants of God, and to whom the help of God has been given, to whom has been granted victory over his enemies, the supporter of truth, the world and the religion, Shāh Rukh Bahādur Khān (may Almighty God make his rule and sultanate abide for ever in the Caliphate over the world, and grant increase of His goodness and blessings for the inhabitants of the earth).' [16]

This ambitious aim finds further literary expression in the work of Shāh Rukh's biographer who speaks of 'his sacred titles being recited on the pulpits of the two Sanctuaries ',[17] an ambition that does not appear to have ever achieved fulfilment. That a mere historian who had enjoyed the patronage of Shāh Rukh should follow such distinguished monarchs, is not to be wondered at, and Ḥāfiẓ Abrū while recounting the praises of his benefactor prays that God may make his Khilāfat and his power endure for ever,[18] and styles him 'the shadow of God, the sultan of the world (may God make his Khilāfat and dominion and power endure for ever).'[19]

But by this period the practice of assuming the title of Khalīfah had become too common for any one individual to attempt to revive the associations of universal sovereignty connected with it in the glorious days of the eighth century, least of all a monarch like Shāh Rukh, whose kinsmen constantly broke out in revolt against him, and the capital of whose dominions, Samarqand, was in the extreme north-west of the historic Muslim empire. Indeed, so many princes, since the destruction of the Abbasid dynasty of Baghdad in 1258, had adopted the habit of styling themselves Khalīfah, that by the reign of Shāh Rukh their number had become quite considerable.

One of the first of such princes to recognize that this supreme title was at the disposal of any one who cared to snatch at it, was Abū 'Abdallāh Muḥammad, of the Ḥafṣid dynasty in Tunis (1249–1277). His father, Yaḥyà, had ruled Tunis as governor for the Almohad of Morocco, but had made himself independent. Ambitious as he was, he had shrunk from taking the supreme title, Amīr ul-Mu'minīn, which belonged to his master the Almohad Khalīfah. His son was bolder and not only styled himself Amīr ul-Mu'minīn, but also Khalīfah and Imām. Whether he did so shortly before, or just after the fall of Baghdad in 1258, is uncertain; the historians are not agreed as to the exact date, but he appears to have been influenced in his decision by a prompting given him by the Sharīf of Mecca. His successors of the Ḥafṣid dynasty continued to bear the same titles.

After an end had been put to the dynasty of the Almohads by the capture of their capital in 1269, Abū 'Īnān Fāris (1348–1358), of the Marīnid dynasty which ruled in Morocco from 1269 to 1470, called himself Amīr ul-Mu'minīn, and Ibn Baṭṭūta, who dedicated his travels to this prince, calls his patron Khalīfah and Amīr ul-Mu'minīn and Imām and Shadow of God upon earth.[20] But few of the other Amīrs of the Marīnid dynasty exhibited similar pretensions.

In Asia Minor, one of the later Saljūqs of Rūm, Ghiyāth ud-Dīn Kay Khusrau III, built a Madrasa at Siwas in the year 1271, and put up an inscription on it, with the prayer: 'O God help Thy servant, Thy Khalīfah, the great Sulṭān, the exalted Khāqān, the lord of the kings of the Arabs and the non-Arabs, the Shadow of God upon earth.'[21]

In India, Sultan 'Alā ud-Dīn Khaljī (1296–1316) of Delhi was styled by his biographer, the great poet Amīr Khusrau, 'the Caliph of his age' and 'the shadow of the Merciful on the heads of mankind'.[22] His son, Quṭb ud-Dīn Mubārak Shāh (1316–1320), had inscribed on some of his coins 'The most exalted Imām, the Khalīfah of the Lord of the worlds, the pole-star of the earth and of the faith, Abu 'l-Muẓaffar Mubārak Shāh', and on others, 'The most exalted Imām, the pole-star of the earth and of the faith, Abu 'l-Muẓaffar,

Khalīfah of God.'[23] About 1382 Aḥmad ibn Uways, one of the last of the Jalā'ir dynasty which had made Baghdad its capital, is described by Dawlatshāh[24] as succeeding his father 'on the seat of the Caliphate' in the ancient capital of the Abbasids. Even Tīmūr (1369–1404), though he appears to have had little regard for the institution of the Caliphate, is described by Niẓām ud-Dīn Shāmī, the historian, whom he commissioned to write the history of his reign and his conquests, as 'the refuge of the Khilāfat' and 'the Shadow of the Merciful'.[25]

In Asia Minor, the initiator of a semi-social, semi-religious movement, Badr ud-Dīn ibn Qāḍī Simāw, who advocated friendship with Christians and proposed to establish a community of goods, when he found his influence growing, assumed the title 'Khalīfah upon earth'; but his power was short-lived, for he came in conflict with the Turkish troops near Smyrna and was put to death in 1417.[26]

Ūzūn Ḥasan, the Sultan of the Turkomans of the White Sheep, who ruled over Diyār Bakr, 'Irāq, Ādharbayjān and Armenia (1453–1477), in a letter he wrote to the Ottoman Sultan Muḥammad II, about the year 1471, describes his capital, Shiraz, which he had recently gained by conquest, as 'the mansion of the seat of the Sultanate and the throne of the Caliphate'.[27] In the introduction to the Akhlāq-i-Jalālī, which was dedicated about the same date to Ūzūn Ḥasan by Jalāl ud-Dīn Dawānī, the author prays for the blessing of God upon his patron, and adds 'May Allāh make the shadow of his Khilāfat abide for ever'.[28]

It was doubtless more flattering to his son Ya'qūb, who was chief of the Turkomans of the White Sheep from 1479 to 1490, to be addressed by the young Ottoman Prince Salīm as 'Your highness, the seat of the Caliphate'.[29]

In another part of the Muslim world, Muḥammad Shaybānī (1500–1510), the founder of the Uzbeg kingdom of Transoxiana, styled himself on his coins 'the Imām of the age, the Khalīfah of the Merciful'.[30] His contemporary, Sultan Ḥusayn, of Khurāsān (who died in 1505), was addressed by so powerful a sovereign as the Ottoman Sultan, Muḥammad II, as 'Your exalted majesty . . . seated by right on the throne of the Khilāfat',[31] and the historian Dawlatshāh, who wrote during his reign, speaks of him as 'adorning the throne of the Khilāfat'.[32] Even some of the later Mamlūk Sultans, though they upheld the institution of the Caliphate in their midst in the person of the Abbasid living under their protection, did not shrink from robbing him of one of his most sacred titles. Thus Sultan Jaqmaq (1438–1453), Qā'it Bay (1468–1495), and Qānṣūh Ghūrī (1500–1516), all put up inscriptions describing themselves as 'the most exalted Imām', thus assuming to themselves the headship of the Muslim world, by the use of a title that had not become so trite as that of Khalīfah.[33]

From the examples given above it is clear that

such assumptions of the titles belonging to the Caliphate were not made in accordance with any regular system; in some cases, it is a sovereign who arrogates to himself a designation that implies he is greater than his contemporaries; in others, one Muslim monarch wishes to pay a compliment to another; in many instances a man of letters wishes to flatter his patron; in others, the language used seems to depend upon the individual caprice of the court scribe. But in every case it is a usurpation, and implies a break with the original theory of the position of the Caliph, according to which he alone was the fountain of honour and alone could bestow titles on lesser monarchs.

How haphazard this ascription of the title of Caliph often was, being left to the whim of the particular scribe or man of letters who is describing his patron, may be judged from the variants to be found sometimes in manuscripts, e.g. in two biographies of Tīmūr, one of which obviously plagiarizes the other, in describing the same event, the one historian refers simply to His Majesty, the other adds to these words 'Protector of the Caliphate'.[34] Again, in a copy of the Iskandarnāmah, in the Bibliothèque Nationale,[35] written in 1390 for a son of Sultan Bāyazīd I, by a Turkish poet Aḥmadī, the scribe has put headings to the sections in which various Muslim princes are described, e.g. 'the Khilāfat of Ghāzān' (fol. 254), 'the Khilāfat of 'Uthmān' (fol. 265), &c., but he goes still farther and ascribes a similar dignity to the ancestors of Ghāzān, e. g. 'the Khilāfat of Abāghā,' and 'the Khilāfat of Gaykhātū' (fol. 252), though these personages were heathens and not Muslims at all. The manuscripts of the same work in the British Museum [36] have in each instance Pādshāhī instead of Khilāfat.

Examples enough have been given to show how widespread had become the practice for any independent sovereign to seek to enhance his dignity by taking on himself the title Khalīfah. To the uncompromising theologian, mindful of the Traditions, such a practice could only appear reprehensible; but more open minds could find for it a justification, and Ibn Khaldūn, taking the view that the office was a vicegerency for the Prophet and that the function of the Caliph was to protect the religion and administer the affairs of the world, recognized that such a vicegerency could be assumed by the Sultans of countries widely separated from one another, when no single person was to be found possessing all the qualities requisite in a Caliph, in the original application of this word.[37]

X

THE EXPOSITION OF PHILOSOPHICAL AND ETHICAL WRITERS

AMONG the influences that contributed towards the adoption in the Muhammadan world of this more widely applicable use of the title Khalīfah, may probably be included the study of Greek political thought. Since the early part of the ninth century when the zeal for the translation of Greek works of philosophy and science burst out in full vigour, the knowledge of this literature had rapidly spread in learned Muhammadan circles. Their interest was primarily in works of metaphysics, logic, mathematics and the physical sciences, but political philosophy and ethics were not neglected. Many of the Muhammadan thinkers attempted to form a synthesis between what they learned from Plato and Aristotle, and the intellectual concepts of Islam; and in the realm of political science they assimilated Aristotle's doctrine of the παμβασιλεύς and the σπουδαῖος ἀνήρ to the Muslim theory of the Khalīfah.

One of the Muslim philosophers who watched the decline of the power of the Abbasids and saw the Caliph become a mere puppet in the hands of his Turkish guards, was al-Fārābī, who died in 950, at the age of about eighty, after living for some time under the protection of one of the princes who had contributed to the break-up of the Arab empire, the Hamdānid Sayf ud-Dawlah. Under the influence of Platonic doctrine, he worked out a theory of an ideal state, governed by philosophers who, comprehending the nature of the first Existence, God, and of the emanations of this first Existence, and of the origin and the course of nature, could guide the soul of man in its effort to return to the source from which it came. Just as the universe is a harmonious whole, under the supreme authority of God, with an orderly sequence of graded existences, and just as the human spirit is made up of successive degrees of intelligence and the human body is an organized whole over which the heart presides, so in like manner the state is an organism or graded system. The ideal state would be under the guidance of a leader who knows what true happiness is, since without the guidance of such a leader man cannot attain his proper goal; this head of the state must possess such virtues as intelligence, loftiness of soul, love of justice, temperance, &c.[1] Al-Fārābī's speculative outlook probably concerned itself little with the actual political condition of the world in which he lived, but it is obvious how such speculations could be applied to the theory of the Caliphate, as soon as it ceased to be regarded merely from a theological point of view.

A group of thinkers, known as the Ikhwān uṣ-Ṣafà, about the latter part of the tenth century, produced an encyclopaedic work dealing with every branch of philosophy, practical as well as theoretical. They more definitely laid down a doctrine of the Caliphate, in harmony with that wider use of the title of Khalīfah, which recognition of the impotency of the Caliph in Baghdad suggested to thoughtful minds, and in this respect the writings of the Ikhwān uṣ-Ṣafà were not possibly without influence on the thought of their co-religionists. They declared that kings are the Caliphs (or vicegerents) of God upon His earth, for He has given them authority over His servants and His territories, in order that they may adjudicate between His creatures with justice and equity, succour the weak, and show mercy to the afflicted; keep in subjection the oppressors, and make men submit to the ordinances of the Law. On the other hand, the judges (the qāḍīs) are the Caliphs (or vicegerents) of the prophets, while the king is the guardian of religion.[2]

The philosophic doctrine was put forward in a more speculative form by Shihāb ud-Dīn Suhrawardī, who was put to death for heresy in Aleppo in 1191, before he had reached the age of 38. In his Ḥikmat ul-Ishrāq, the philosophy of illumination, he approaches the problem of government from a point of view in many respects Platonic. The world (he says) has never been wholly without philosophy, or without a man who practices it and is indicated as such by manifest proofs and signs; he is then the Khalīfah and will remain so as long as Heaven and Earth endure. There are various degrees of philosophic and theosophic knowledge;

if complete mastery in both these forms of wisdom is bound in one person, then he is Khalīfah of God upon earth. If no such person exists, then this exalted designation belongs to the complete theosophist, for the speculative philosopher who is not at the same time a theosophist has no rightful claim to it. Writing as a Sufi, Suhrawardī is careful to explain that by this Khilāfat is not to be understood worldly power, for the authority that goes along with this high dignity may belong to a man, even though he lives in the deepest poverty, and may be exercised by him secretly; if, however, power comes to him and he assumes this authority openly, then is the world filled with light; otherwise it is full of darkness.[3]

These philosophic representations of the Khalīfah, as being the enlightened and just ruler, were popularized in the numerous manuals, written especially in Persian and embellished by illustrative anecdotes, for the guidance of princes, and compiled in a simple form, fitted to the limited intelligences of the various barbarous princes who broke up the Arab empire into separate kingdoms. One of the earliest of these, written in Arabic in the tenth or eleventh century, though commonly said to have been translated from the Greek by Yuḥannā ibn Bitrīq in the early part of the ninth century, claimed to contain the advice which Aristotle gave to his pupil Alexander on justice and the various duties of a king, political organization, the waging of war, &c. The great minister of the Saljūqs, Niẓām ul-Mulk, compiled such a treatise on the art of government about the year 1092, which he dedicated to Sultan Malikshāh. This is not a philosophical treatise expounding a political theory, but is made up mainly of practical advice as to methods of administration, the giving of audience, the execution of justice, and the watchful superintendence of various functionaries, military, judicial, and financial, whose conduct was to be constantly reported to the king by his spies. But in it he enunciates the doctrine of kingship that was gaining wide acceptance in this period, and writes, 'In every age God selects a man whom He adorns with kingly qualities and to whom He entrusts the well-being and the peace of His servants.' [4]

There is more philosophic depth and more systematic treatment of political problems in the Akhlāq-i-Nāṣirī, so styled after the name of its compiler, Naṣīr ud-Dīn Ṭūsī (*ob.* 1274), one of the most active writers of religious and philosophical books in the thirteenth century. As he was in the service of Hūlāgū, and on account of his knowledge of astronomy was consulted by this Mongol sovereign as to whether the stars were favourable for the undertaking of any enterprise, and as he accompanied Hūlāgū at the siege of Baghdad and persuaded him that no divine vengeance was likely to follow the death of the Caliph, he naturally lays no particular emphasis on a political institution which he was willing to see so ruthlessly destroyed. Moreover, Naṣīr ud-Dīn was a Shiah, and therefore had little interest in giving an exposition of the Sunnī doctrine of the Caliphate; but he identified the Imām with the ideal ruler as described by Plato and Aristotle.

This work served as the basis of what later on became one of the most popular manuals of ethics wherever the Persian language was read, the Akhlāq-i-Jalālī of Jalāl ud-Dīn Dawānī, compiled about 1470 and dedicated to Ūzūn Ḥasan, the chief of the Turkomans of the White Sheep, to whom reference has already frequently been made. He was strongly influenced by Aristotelian philosophy in the form in which it had by this time been made widely known in the Muhammadan world by Muhammadan thinkers themselves, but Jalāl ud-Dīn presents this political speculation in a more distinctively Muhammadan form than is found in the writings of some of his predecessors. He quotes the well-known verses of the Qur'ān (vi. 165 and xxxviii. 25) which occur so frequently in the literature of this period, and lays it down that it is the first duty of the administrator of the world to uphold the authority of the Muslim law, and then he is indeed the Shadow of God and the Khalīfah of God and the Lieutenant of the Prophet.

It would therefore appear that since the supreme power had passed out of the hands of the Abbasids, Arabs of the tribe of the Quraysh, and had b en assumed by various princes of barbarous origin, for whom no such exalted genealogy could be adduced, it was necessary for the salving of tender consciences to find some other justification of the obedience which the pious Muslim was called upon to show to his new rulers ; this had been done by concentrating attention on the words of the Qur'ān, which gave to the title Khalīfah a more general reference ; and now philosophy was brought in to uphold the same position. This assistance had been rendered more easily possible from the fact that from the twelfth century onwards, after a long struggle between the theologians and the unorthodox philosophers, philosophy had been taken into the curriculum of Muslim theological studies, being presented in modified forms held to be in harmony with the fundamental doctrines of Islam. Even those who were not professed students of philosophy felt the influence of such an appeal to a reasoned exposition of political theory, and combined it with the more popular method of appeal to the Word of God. Thus the historian, Ḥāfiẓ Abrū, writing the praises of his patron Shāh Rukh, says, ' It has been established by decisive proofs and by clear arguments that after the great law (that is, the exalted Sharī'ah) there is no order or rank more dignified than dominion and sultanate, and what rank or status could be higher, since God (glorious is His majesty and sublime is His Word) has in His eternal Word appointed just kings to be Caliphs and Lieutenants of Himself, and has placed in the hand of their choice and the grasp of their will the reins of work and action, in that he says that it is He who makes you Caliphs upon earth and lifts up some above others in rank, and the Prophet (the blessing of the Merciful be upon him) has borne witness to the truth of this doctrine and the soundness of this claim, and some have interpreted power (sulṭān) as being the Shadow of God upon earth, and all those who are oppressed take refuge with him.'[5]

XI

THE OTTOMANS AND THE CALIPHATE

THE title of Khalīfah seems during this period to have assumed a new significance; it certainly no longer implied descent from the house of ‘Abbas or any claim to belong to the tribe of the Quraysh. The Muslim monarch now claimed to derive his authority directly from God, to be the vicegerent of Allāh, not a mere successor of the Prophet; and the other designations, such as Imām and Amīr ul-Mu'minīn, that had hitherto been associated with the Caliphate, generally dropped into abeyance, and were rarely assumed by those who called themselves Caliphs. The frequent quotation of the verses (Qur'ān, xxxviii. 25) ‘And we have made thee a Khalīfah (vicegerent) on the earth’, and (Qur'ān, vi. 165) ‘He hath made you Caliphs on the earth’ in the official documents of this period,[1] to the virtual exclusion of any other Qur'ānic verse or any Tradition that had been commonly adduced by theologians of an earlier age when dealing with the Khilāfat, points to the same conclusion; it was from God and God alone that these rulers derived their authority and in such verses He Himself announced their appointment as His vicegerents. Thus the title of Caliph passed from the supreme authority who used to nominate Sultans, to any Sultan who cared to assume a designation once held to be unique. When so many lesser princes in the Muhammadan world were arrogating to themselves this exalted title, it is hardly surprising to find that it was not refused to the rising power of the Ottoman Sultans, and since many of their correspondents attributed to them this dignity in various forms of address, the flattery was presumably not unwelcome to them. Murād I was frequently so styled; when he had conquered Adrianople, Philippopolis and other cities (about 1362), the Amīr of Karamania in Asia Minor wrote to congratulate him on his victories and described him as 'the chosen Khalīfah of the Creator' and 'the shadow of God upon earth'.[2] In his reply Murād gives utterance to the pious sentiment that there is no difference in nature or substance between ruler and subject, but that God has bestowed upon some of his chosen servants the dignity of the Caliphate, in order that taking upon themselves this heavy responsibility, they may relieve the misery of the helpless; and he calls upon God to witness that from the date of his coming to the throne he had not taken a moment's rest, but had devoted himself day and night to waging war and jihād, and always had his armour on to serve the Muslim weal; so that any one who prayed that he (Murād) might be victorious, would thereby serve his own advantage.[3] It is clear from this letter that Murād regarded himself as a Caliph, of course in the sense of this word as understood by his contemporaries.

A similar letter of congratulation, sent by

another Amīr of Asia Minor, Isfandiyār Beg, of Qasṭamūnī, in 1374, addresses Murād as 'Your Highness who has attained the pre-eminent rank of the Caliphate, . . . Sultan of the Sultans of Islam, and Khāqān of the Khāqāns of mankind'.[4] In the following year a letter from the governor of Erzerum describes him as 'the lord of the world, whose under-garment is the Caliphate'.[5]

The capture of Nish, one of the furthest points of Murād's victorious campaigns on the high road to Hungary, after a siege of twenty-five days in 1375, was the occasion of another letter of congratulation—this time from 'Alī Beg of Karamania, who expresses his delight at this victory of 'the ornament of the throne of the Caliphate' and prays that 'God Almighty may stablish the pillars of his Caliphate until the judgement day'.[6]

The aggressive attitude of his son and successor, Bāyazīd I (1389–1402), towards the Amīrs of Asia Minor was not calculated to induce them to bestow on him titles implying the headship of the Muhammadan world, and his more powerful rivals such as the Mamlūk Sultan of Egypt and (for a time) Sultan Aḥmad Jalā'ir of 'Iraq appear to have regarded his military successes and the extension of his territories as constituting a grave menace to their own safety. Least of all, was his most serious rival, Tīmūr, who later achieved his ruin and took him prisoner after the disastrous battle of Angora (1402), ready to pay him compliments, and the bitter tone of their correspondence left no room for the mellifluous elegancies of diplomatic phraseology; indeed, the acrimony of it reached such a point that, instead of a long enumeration of titles and invocations of divine blessing, Tīmūr bluntly addresses (probably about 1401) his rival with the words, 'O King in Rūm, Yildirim Bāyazīd.' [7] But Bāyazīd when, about the end of November 1395, he published the news of his victories to the qāḍīs and other officials of his kingdom did not hesitate to write to them: 'God has fitted me whose nature bears the marks of the Caliphate, to be a sultan and a world-conqueror, and has set (His words) "We have made thee a Khalīfah on the earth" in my royal cipher and device.' [8]

When Bāyazīd died as a prisoner in the hands of Tīmūr, the Ottoman state seemed on the verge of ruin; his sons fought with one another for his inheritance, and the kingdom was for a time divided into three parts, each governed by an independent Sultan, claiming to be the sole heir of his father. It was not until ten years after his father's death that Muḥammad I in 1413 defeated the last of his rivals and was able to take up the task of restoring order in the distracted Ottoman dominions. In his letters bearing the intelligence of his success in 1415 to contemporary Muhammadan potentates, such as Shamsuddīn Muḥammad, the Amīr of Karamania, Hamzah Beg (son of the governor of Smyrna), who had come to his aid opportunely with a troop of horsemen a few years before, on the eve of his final conflict with his brother Mūsà,[9] and to the qāḍī of Brusa,[10] Muḥammad I makes no claim to the title of Khalīfah, but he soon adopted the fashion of his fathers and in 1416 in a letter to Shāh Rukh speaks of 'affairs of his Sultanate and Caliphate'; [11] and in a letter to Qara Yūsuf, the Turkoman Sultan of the Black Sheep (the Qara-Qoyūnlū), about 1418, he describes his capital as 'the abode of the Khilāfat'.[12] Nor did he lack those who would flatter him with such exalted terms of address; about 1417 Qara Iskandar, the son (and afterwards successor) of the above-mentioned Qara Yūsuf, who at that time ruled over the greater part of Persia and 'Iraq, addressed him as 'the sun in the sign of the Khilāfat'.[13] About the same period, the governor of the province of Shīrwān, Sulṭān Khalīl, invented for him the strange appellation of 'the index of the book of the Sultanate and the preface of the (divine) message of the Caliphate', by which he implied that Muḥammad I was both Sultan and Khalīfah.[14]

The recognition which his son Murād II received on his accession in 1421 was immediate; Jahān Shāh Mīrzā, brother of the Qara Qoyūnlū prince, Iskandar, who had acknowledged the Caliphate of Muḥammad I, exhausted the resources of the Persian language in his letter of congratulation to Murād on his ascending the throne of his father; after declaring that God bestows the robe of honour of the Caliphate and the cloak of the Sultanate on one of the chosen of the sons of Adam, some incomparable being out of the select among exalted nations, he goes on to address Murād as 'his majesty who has attained to the pre-eminent rank of the Caliphate, the refuge of the Sultanate', and so on, with line after line in praise of his greatness and his prowess on behalf of Islam, ending with the prayer, 'May God Almighty multiply the days of his Sultanate and increase the years of his life and his Caliphate until the day of judgement.'[15]

In acknowledging the receipt of this letter Murād refers to it as having been written from the 'throne of glory and the Caliphate'—thus returning the compliment to Jahān Shāh Mīrzā, by recognizing that he too could claim this title.[16]

But a much more exalted potentate, son of the ruthless conqueror who had inflicted such humiliation on Murād's grandfather—Shāh Rukh—was ready to address the new Sultan in equally flattering terms as 'Your majesty, the seat of the Sultanate and the refuge of the Caliphate (may God Almighty make your Caliphate and your power (sulṭān) endure for ever,—(God) the Writer of the decree "He hath made you Caliphs on the earth", Who hath proclaimed in your illustrious name the Caliphate of the whole world).'[17] Not so impressive is the tribute of respect from Hamzah Beg, chief of the Turkomans of the White Sheep, but as he ruled over Adharbayjan and Diyar Bakr, it is noteworthy that he too prays God may perpetuate for ever the dominion and the power (sulṭān) and the Caliphate of Murād and exalt his dignity above the heavens.[18] Similarly the governor of Mardin, Nāṣir ud-Dīn, when about 1439 he submits a report of his military successes, addresses Murād II as 'the Sultan of the Sultans of the Turks and the Arabs and the Persians, the star of the Khilāfat . . . the shadow of the mercy of God'.[19]

If any Sultan of the Ottoman house might fittingly have received the highest title that the Muhammadan world could bestow, it was surely Muḥammad II, the Conqueror, after he had established the capital of the Turkish empire in Constantinople (that great Christian city which had foiled all Muslim attempts to take it by storm for nearly eight centuries). One of the most formidable of contemporary Muhammadan sovereigns, who was soon to become a troublesome rival of the Ottoman power and was consequently courted by the Christian states of Venice and Trebizond in their fear of increasing aggression on the part of the Turks—Ūzūn Ḥasan, the greatest monarch of the dynasty of the Turkomans of the White Sheep—writing an account of his conquest of Adharbayjan and 'Iraq to Muḥammad II in 1467, prayed that God might make Muḥammad's dominion and Caliphate and power (sulṭān) abide for ever throughout the whole earth and cause his justice and mercy and kindness to be poured forth over the world.[20] Another letter from the same prince, written a little later to report further military successes, addresses Muḥammad II as 'the light of the pupil of the eye of the Caliphate '.[21] As their rivalry became more pronounced, Ūzūn Ḥasan dropped these complimentary phrases and adopted an insolent tone in his correspondence.

Muḥammad does not appear to have used the title of Khalīfah in his own correspondence either with contemporary sovereigns or with his own subjects—with the strange exception of his sons; Muṣṭafà, in 1482, he styles ' light of the pupil of the eye of the Sultanate and light of the garden of the Caliphate ',[22] and uses a variant of the same phrase for his ill-fated son Jem, at the time when he was governor of Qasṭamūnī, ' light of the garden of the Sultanate and light of the pupil of the eye of the Caliphate.' [23]

Friendly relations existed between his successor, Bāyazīd II (1481–1512) and Ya'qūb, son of that Ūzūn Ḥasan whose hostilities to the Ottoman house have already been referred to; he obviously wished to stand well with Bāyazīd and among the terms of eulogy he lavishes upon him, he includes ' his majesty who has attained the pre-eminent rank of the Caliphate, . . . the glory of the Sultans of the world, seated by right on the throne of the Caliphate '.[24] A nephew of this same prince, named Rustam, addressed Bāyazīd II in similar terms as ' his majesty who has attained the pre-eminent rank of the Caliphate, . . . seated by right on the throne of the Sultanate and exalting the seat of the Caliphate '.[25]

So the claim to the title of Khalīfah descended

from father to son in the Ottoman ruling family until the reign of Salīm I (1512–1520). Before he came to the throne and while he was still a prince, the same chief of the Turkomans of the White Sheep, Sultan Ya'qūb, who had recognized the Caliphate of his father Bāyazīd II, styled Salīm 'the manifestation of the lights of the Caliphate' and 'the right hand of the realm and the justice and the Caliphate,'[26] and in another letter 'the spreading tree of the garden of the Caliphate, . . . Sultan Salīm Shāh (may God lengthen the days of his power and the years of his felicity in the shadow of the Caliphate of his august father)'.[27] Similarly, while Salīm was still a prince, he received from Abu'l-Muẓaffar, Shāh of Alwand, a letter describing him as 'the choicest of Sultans, whose under-garment is the Caliphate, . . . the greatest of the most eminent holders of the Caliphate, . . . who lifteth up the flags of Islam to the sky of glory, the stay of the Sultanate and of justice, the right hand of the Caliphate, Sultan Salīm (may God cause the pillars of his prosperity to abide . . . in the shadow of his majesty, his august father, the Caliph of the Merciful among the faithful, may God make the shadow of his imperial Caliphate abide for ever)'.[28] Salīm must therefore, long before he himself came to the throne, have been accustomed to regard the Caliphate as an apanage of the royal Ottoman family, and to have been well aware that his father was saluted as Caliph, even as his grandfather and many another ancestor had been so styled before him. When in November 1512, his brother Qūrqūd made his submission to the new Sultan, he describes Salīm as ‘ laying the foundations of the columns of empire and firmly building up the pillars of the Caliphate . . . the Shadow of God upon earth’.[29]

It is commonly stated that Sultan Salīm assumed the title of Caliph after his conquest of Egypt, when in Cairo the last Abbasid Caliph, Mutawakkil, solemnly transferred it to him, but as early as 1514 Salīm had already styled himself ‘ the Khalīfah of God throughout the length and breadth of the earth ’,[30] and he had been saluted (along with other high-sounding titles) as ‘ he who attained the exalted rank of the Caliphate ’ by contemporary princes before the Egyptian campaign had been planned, e.g. by Sultan ‘Ubayd Allāh Khān, the Uzbeg ruler of Samarqand, who in August 1514 (apparently before he had heard of the victory at Chāldirān) answered a letter that Sultan Salīm had sent him in the previous January,[31] and by Shāh Ismā‘īl, in a letter written after the battle of Chāldirān (August 1514), in which he was so completely defeated ;[32] and in two congratulatory poems on the victory of Chāldirān, Khwājah Isfahānī lauds him as ‘ Caliph of God and of Muḥammad ’[33] and as ‘ king of the throne of the Caliphate ’.[34] Further, Salīm refers in a similar manner to himself, when, informing his son Sulaymān of the victory at Chāldirān, he begins ‘ Beloved son . . . light of the pupil of the eye of the Sultanate and victorious light of the garden of the Caliphate’.[35]

XII

SULTAN SALĪM IN EGYPT

By his crushing defeat of the Persians at Chāldirān in 1514 and his subsequent annexation of Kurdistan and Diyar-Bakr, Salīm had effectually checked the growing power of Shāh Ismā'īl and was for a time safe from the aggressive policy of his ambitious rival on the eastern borders of the Ottoman dominions. He was now free to turn his arms against the Mamlūks of Egypt, with whom he had a long outstanding quarrel. Egyptian troops had on more than one occasion during his father's reign invaded Asia Minor and celebrated their victories with long lines of captives led in triumph through Cairo. Rival claimants to the Ottoman throne found a welcome in Egypt, and there was little doubt that the sympathies of the Mamlūk Sultan had been with Shah Ismā'īl in the conflict between Persia and Turkey, but the favourable opportunity for active assistance had been allowed to slip by, and now that Salīm had come out victorious, the Mamlūk prince became not unnaturally alarmed, and spent the winter of 1515 and the spring of 1516 in equipping an army for the great struggle.

In May 1516 the Egyptian army under the command of the Sultan Qānṣūh Ghūrī left Egypt, accompanied by the Abbasid Caliph and the four chief Qāḍīs. In August he was defeated by Salīm at Marj Dābiq near Aleppo; Qānṣūh was killed; Salīm occupied Aleppo and pitched his camp outside the city; here he received the Caliph, who had been taken prisoner after the battle of Dābiq, and the account of the interview seems to suggest that Salīm made him recognize his inferior status;[1] he asked him what was his place of origin; when the Caliph answered, 'Baghdad', Salīm said, 'Then we will send you back again to Baghdad'. He gave the Caliph a robe of honour and a present of money, and let him return to Aleppo. At the end of September Salīm entered Damascus and the Caliph followed him there two days later. Salīm stayed in Damascus for over two months.

Meanwhile, a new Sultan, Tūmān Bay, had to be appointed in Cairo, and for this ceremony the presence of the Caliph was necessary. The father of Mutawakkil, Mustamsik (who had resigned the office of Caliph in 1509 on account of old age), came forward and performed the ceremony as representative of his son in October 1516.

In December Salīm set out on his march to Egypt; the outposts of the Egyptian army were beaten at Gaza on the 19th December, and the main army of Tūmān Bay defeated at Rīdānia, in the neighbourhood of Cairo, on 22nd January 1517, and on the following day the Khuṭbah was read in the name of Salīm in the mosques of Cairo. 'O God, give victory to the Sultan, son of the Sultan, the king of the two continents and the two seas, the destroyer of the two armies, the Sultan of the two 'Irāqs, the servant of the two Holy Sanctuaries, the victorious King, Sultan Salīm Shāh.' [2]

On the following Tuesday, Tūmān Bay forced his way into the city; for three days there was fighting in the streets, and on the Friday the Khuṭbah was read in the name of Tūmān Bay. But on the very same day, Salīm succeeded in driving the Mamlūks out of the city, and Tūmān Bay fled into Upper Egypt. Negotiations passed between the two monarchs, and the Caliph was the recipient of Tūmān Bay's letter to Salīm, and Salīm wanted the Caliph and the four Qāḍīs to be the bearers of his reply; but the Caliph declined and sent a deputy instead. Tūmān Bay collected another army, but at the end of March was defeated near the Pyramids by the Ottomans, and treacherously given up to Salīm a few days later, and put to death in April.

For a few months Salīm appears to have allowed the Caliph to exercise a certain amount of authority in the administration, and his palace was consequently crowded with petitioners who sought his intercession on their behalf. Salīm doubtless found it politic to make use of his prisoner in this manner, in order to reconcile the populace of Cairo to the new government. During this brief period Mutawakkil is said to have received more presents than ever his ancestors received before him and this accession of fortune quite turned his head; [3]

but the unfortunate Caliph was soon undeceived, for in June Salīm banished him to Constantinople. They did not meet again until a year later, when Salīm himself returned to Constantinople in July 1518. At first the Sultan appears to have shown him some consideration, but his attitude towards him soon changed ; the Caliph quarrelled with his relatives over the division of their allowance, and appears to have been shamefully extravagant, especially in buying dancing girls for his amusement.[4] Salīm became so annoyed that he imprisoned him in a castle, where he probably remained until after Salīm's death in September 1520. In the reign of Sulaymān, according to the historian Quṭb ud-Dīn, who made his acquaintance in Cairo in 1536, Mutawakkil returned to Cairo and 'became Khalīfah there',[5] and in the year 1523 once more exercised his old function of investing a Sultan of Egypt, as his ancestors had done before him, when the governor Aḥmad Pasha revolted against Sultan Sulaymān and for a brief period made himself independent.[6] This is the last recorded act of Mutawakkil, but he continued to live on in Cairo until his death in 1543.

The popular account at the present day of the relations between Sultan Salīm and the Khalīfah Mutawakkil is that the Caliph made a formal transfer of his office to the conqueror, and as a symbol of this transference handed over to him the sacred relics, which were believed to have come down from the days of the Prophet—the robe, of which mention has already been made as being worn by the Abbasids of Baghdad on solemn state occasions—some hairs from his beard, and the sword of the Caliph 'Umar. There is no doubt that Salīm carried off these reputed relics to Constantinople (where they are still preserved in the mosque of Ayyūb), as part of the loot which he acquired by the conquest of Egypt; but of the alleged transfer of the dignity of the Khilāfat there is no contemporary evidence at all.

There are two contemporary accounts of the campaign which terminated in the conquest of Egypt, giving in the form of a diary a record of what happened day by day—apparently the official reports drawn up by the court chronicler; [7] two Turkish and one Persian historian were eye-witnesses of this triumph of Sultan Salīm and wrote a narrative of it from personal knowledge; [8] but none of these contemporary sources make any reference whatsoever to any such transfer, indeed they appear to have regarded the unfortunate relic of the Abbasid dynasty as unworthy of their notice. For such information as we have of Mutawakkil's position during this period we are indebted to an Egyptian scholar, Ibn Iyās, who appears to have been well-informed and to have been interested in the fate of the Abbasid Caliph; though he gives many details, there is not the slightest indication of such a transfer of his high office, and even after Mutawakkil had been banished to Constantinople, Ibn Iyās refers to this city merely as ‘ the seat of the throne of the Ottoman kingdom ’.[9]

It is noteworthy also that in the letter[10] which Sultan Salīm wrote to his son Prince Sulaymān, giving in detail the various triumphs of his campaign, culminating in the conquest of Egypt, he makes no mention whatsoever of the Khalīfah. If such a transference of an office, once believed to be the most exalted in the Muslim world, had actually taken place, and if Sultan Salīm had cared at all for the title of ‘ Khalīfah ’, it seems incredible that he should not have made mention of it in such an enumeration of his successes. For it is clear from this letter to Sulaymān, giving a detailed account of the campaign from the battle of Marj Dābiq to the conquest of Egypt, that what he prided himself on was the immense extension of territory that his victory had brought him. ‘ Praise be to God, the Lord of the worlds, now the whole length and breadth of the territories of Egypt—Malatiyah and Aleppo and holy Damascus and Cairo itself and Upper Egypt and Abyssinia and the Yaman to the frontier of Qayrawan in the west—and the Hijaz and Mecca and Yathrib and Medina and Jerusalem—have all been comprised within the Ottoman territories, and Sayyid Abu'l-Ḥasan, the young son of the Sharīf Abu'l-Barakāt ibn Sharīf Muḥammad, is going to come to the foot of my world-embracing throne.’[11] There is definite historical evidence that he was overjoyed at having acquired the right to style himself 'Servant of the two Holy Sanctuaries'—a title that had been held by the Mamlūk Sultan, and not by the Abbasid Caliph—for when, after the death of his rival in the battle of Marj Dābiq, he could assume this coveted title, and in January 1517 he heard himself described in the Khuṭbah in the great mosque of Aleppo as 'Servant of the two Holy Sanctuaries', he bowed himself down in thanksgiving to God and gave vent to the joy and satisfaction he felt, and bestowed robes of honour on the preacher in the pulpit.[12] But by this period the title of Khalīfah had been assumed by so many insignificant princes that it had ceased to carry with it the same impressive associations as it had borne in earlier centuries, and Salīm was probably not unaware of the fact that when his hated rival, the Shah of Persia, had a few years before, in 1508, taken Baghdad from the Turkomans, he put in a eunuch as governor of the old imperial city, with the title of 'Caliph of the Caliphs'.[13]

Moreover, as has been pointed out above, Salīm and his ancestors had already long been accustomed to enjoy such prestige as went along with the use of the title Khalīfah, and when Salīm cared to adopt it, he would do so, as his fathers had done before him, in virtue of divine appointment, and he would certainly not look upon himself as having taken it over from so insignificant and so negligible a personage as the Abbasid Caliph of Cairo, in whose family the historic Caliphate had lost all the dignity that it had once possessed, in consequence of the degraded position to which its representatives had been reduced during the two centuries and a half of subserviency to Mamlūk caprice. If reference had to be made to any family that had enjoyed this high honour, it was his own, that of the Ottoman Sultans, and he does so refer to it as 'this family that has been the abode of the Caliphate' in a letter written to the governor of Māzandarān, in December 1517—months after the last Abbasid Caliph had been sent into exile to Constantinople.[14]

The fiction that the last Abbasid Caliph of Egypt handed over his dignity, by a formal act of transfer, to Sultan Salīm, was first enunciated in 1787 by Constantine Mouradgea d'Ohsson in his monumental work, *Tableau général de l'Empire Othoman.** He supported this statement by refer-

* After quoting the principle that the Imām must be of the Quraysh, he goes on: 'La maison Othomane n'a pas l'avantage d'être du même sang, comme l'exige la loi canonique, pour avoir droit à l'Imameth. Cependant, selon l'opinion unanime des juristes modernes, ce droit est acquis aux Sultans Othomans, par la renonciation formelle qu'en fit, l'an 923 (1517), en faveur de cette maison souveraine, dans la personne de Selim I, Mohammed XII Ebu-Djeafer, dit Mutewwekil al' allah. C'est le dernier des Khaliphes Abassides, dont le sacerdoce fut détruit du même coup qui renversa la puissance des Memlouks Circasses en Égypte. Selim I reçut encore dans la même année les hommages du Schérif de la Mecque, Mohammed Eb'ul-Berekeath, qui lui fit présenter dans un plat d'argent les clefs du Keabé par Ebu-Noumy son fils. Cette cession pleine et entière des droits de l'Imameth, faite d'un côté par un Khaliphe Abasside, et de l'autre par un

ence to no historical source, nor apparently did any of the historians who have since accepted his authority, make any attempt to test the validity of this assertion,[15] and so it has passed unchallenged from one historical work to another—Oriental as well as European—and has become a commonplace in the modern propagandist literature of the Muhammadan world in support of the Ottoman claims to the Caliphate.

We may judge of the description of himself that Salīm himself preferred, from the language of the Khuṭbah that was read in the mosques of Cairo, on the day of his great triumph, 23rd January 1517 (see above, p. 140). Sultan is the title repeated again and again in this Khuṭbah ; by this title the Ottoman historians are accustomed to describe their sovereigns when they refer to them simply, without a string of grandiloquent appellations ; and on his coins Salīm put no other title, as had been the general usage of his forefathers before him ; his father, Bāyazīd II (1481–1512), had introduced the formula, 'Lord of might and victory by land and sea' ; his great-grandson, Murād III (1574–1595), replaced this by the formula, 'Sultan of the two continents, Khāqān of the two seas', and Maḥmūd II (1808–1839)

Schérif de la Mecque, tous deux descendans des Coureyschs, l'un par la branche de Haschim, l'autre par celle d'Aly, supplée, dans les Sultans Othomans, au défaut de la naissance ou de l'extraction qu'exige la loi pour exercer d'une manière légitime les fonctions du sacerdoce' (i. 269–70, ed. 8vo, Paris, 1788–1824).

introduced the variant, 'Sultan of the sultans of the age'. But none of the Ottomans described themselves on their coins as Khalīfah, or Imām, or Amīr al-Mu'minīn, as they would have done, had they followed the usage of the Abbasid Caliphs or had looked upon themselves as continuing the line of this august dynasty.

It was by the sword, or rather by his cannon, that Salīm had achieved greatness, and his conquests had made him more powerful than any contemporary Muhammadan sovereign, and his empire included territories over which no Khalīfah before him had ever exercised authority. It could hardly have enhanced his reputation in the eyes of the Muslim world for him to have represented himself as the successor of the Abbasid Caliphs of Cairo, whom most of his co-religionists had ignored for generations; on the other hand, by the incorporation of the holy cities of Mecca and Medina within his dominions, he attained a pre-eminence that appealed to every Muhammadan throughout the world. The appearance of the Portuguese in eastern waters was a menace to more than one Muhammadan state, and their raids upon the coast-towns of the Red Sea threatened the safety of the pilgrims to Mecca, and there was reason to fear that the King of Portugal's ambition was the destruction of the Holy City.[16] But now the most powerful and most wealthy monarch in the Muslim world came forward as the Servant of the holy

Sanctuaries and gained thereby the admiration and the grateful prayers of every true believer, even as he excited alarm in the Christian world.

For some centuries past when there had been so many Muslim sovereigns who had not considered it necessary to apply to the Caliph for authorization of their position, their relationship to the holy cities of Mecca and Medina had acquired a new significance. It appears as if such sovereigns, aware of the weakness of their position in respect of the requirements of Muslim law, desired to strengthen their status in the eyes of their Muslim subjects by ostentatious piety and by lavishing rich gifts upon these two holy sanctuaries. From the very outset of the Muhammadan era there had been a connexion between Mecca and Medina and the Caliphate; but, whereas in later times it had come to be believed that one justification for claiming the title 'Khalīfah' was based on the protection of these two holy cities, no such importance appears, in some of the earlier periods of Muslim history, to have been attached to such a protectorate. That the Caliphate could be held by a sovereign who did not include Mecca within the circle of his rule, may be judged by the fact that during the reigns of the Umayyad Caliphs, Yazīd and 'Abd ul-Malik, that is from 681 to 692, there was a rival Khalīfah in Mecca in the person of 'Abdallāh ibn Zubayr. Further, from 930 to 950, Mecca was occupied by the heretic Carmathians, and from 1238 to 1250 it was under the rule of the Rasūlid dynasty of the Yaman. The sack of Mecca in 930 by the Carmathians, who carried off the Black Stone and did not restore it until 950, made the Muslim world realize how helpless the Abbasid Caliph in Baghdad was when protection was needed for the Holy City. A rivalry made itself apparent from this period, as to who should be the protector of the Holy City. From 918 the Fatimid Khilāfat (founded in Mahdiyyah in 909) tried to enhance its status by such a protectorate; but it was not until 969 (the year in which Egypt was added to the Fatimid empire) that the Fatimid Caliph was mentioned in the Friday prayer in Mecca to the exclusion of the Abbasid; and when (e.g. in 976) Mecca was recalcitrant, threats were made of starving it into submission, for it was dependent on Egypt for its supplies of corn. Saladin retained this privilege for the Ayyūbid dynasty he founded in Egypt (1169), and the Mamlūk Sultans continued it (from 1260), though Yaman at times disputed it.

But when the newly established Mongol power accepted Islam, the Mongol Khans also tried to obtain recognition for themselves in Mecca. Abū Sa'īd, the Īlkhān of Persia (1316–1335), successfully intrigued with one of the rival sons of Abū Namayy, the Grand Sharīf of Mecca, who had died in 1301, and in 1318 succeeded in getting his own name inserted in the Khuṭbah in place of that of Nāṣir, the Sultan of Egypt, but Egyptian troops soon succeeded in putting a stop to this intrusion on the part of the Mongol prince.[17]

About a century later, it is quite possible that Tīmūr's ambition included the desire to exercise control over Mecca, for in 1400 he fell out with the Mamlūk Sultan of Egypt, Faraj, led his armies into Syria, which was at that time under Egyptian rule, and captured one city after another, ending with Damascus. To this period probably belongs the undated letter which Tīmūr wrote to Bāyazīd I, protesting against the assumption of the title of 'Sultan of the two Holy Sanctuaries' by the ruler of Egypt, on the ground that Mecca was the Sanctuary of God, and Medina was the Sanctuary of the grave of Muḥammad—and what prouder glory or higher felicity was possible than to be named the custodian and servant of these two Sanctuaries?[18] It was in accordance with the ambitious schemes of his son, Shāh Rukh, for recognition in the Muhammadan world, that in 1444 he applied to the Mamlūk Sultan, Jaqmaq, for a permission that his predecessor Barsbay had already once refused, viz. to send through Egypt a covering for the Ka'bah.[19]

It was probably due to the special fact that the chief of the Turkomans of the Black Sheep (to whom reference has so often been made), Qara Yūsuf, was in occupation of the ancient capital of the Caliphate, Baghdad, and could thereby facilitate the journey of the pilgrims from 'Iraq, that during the pilgrimage of the year 1414 prayers were offered for him in Mecca, but the historian expressly states that these prayers were offered in the evening in the course of the prayers that customarily follow the completion of a reading of the Qur'ān. So Qara Yūsuf did not have the satisfaction of having his name mentioned in the Khuṭbah, delivered in the morning service of the same day, for that would have implied a recognition of sovereignty or at least of nominal headship of the Muslim world.[20]

Devotion to the Holy City had thus become a symbol of distinction in the Muslim world, at a period when the dignity of the Caliph had sunk into insignificance. Whoever was ruler of Egypt could control the fate of Mecca, because he could starve the city out by cutting off the supplies of grain. It was therefore only natural that the Amīr (or Sharīf) of Mecca should tender his submission to Sultan Salīm after he had made his victorious entry into Cairo in 1517, and no religious significance is to be attached to his having sent his son—a boy of twelve—'to tread on the carpet of the Sultan in Egypt'.[21] The boy had visited Cairo four years earlier when Qānṣūh Ghūrī had invited the Sharīf of Mecca to visit him; but having been once before enticed away from Mecca and imprisoned in Egypt, the Sharīf was too astute to run this risk a second time, and so sent his heir, this child of eight, in his place, and apparently the substitution gave no offence, for it so happened that Qānṣūh Ghūrī interpreted a chance word that the boy let drop as a sign of good omen for victory over the Ottomans.[22] So it was to Salīm, as ruler of Egypt, not as any religious or spiritual functionary, that the Sharīf of Mecca made his submission. The Ottoman Sultans had, for several generations past, shown great liberality towards the Holy City, and it was doubtless in anticipation of such gifts in the future—a hope that was not disappointed—that their accession to power was now welcomed, and prayers were offered during the solemn rites of the pilgrimage for 'Sultan Salīm Khān',[23] for having, since the tragedy of 1258, discontinued the mention of the name of any Khalīfah in the Khuṭbah (with the exception above referred to),* the authorities in Mecca apparently did not consider that any new circumstance had arisen to justify a change in their practice.

As explained above, Salīm had been accustomed to be regarded as Caliph from his youth upwards, and must have been aware of the fact that the title had been applied to his father and his ancestors for a century and a half; it was therefore natural that such an appellation should continue to be employed throughout his reign, but it is noticeable that even after the conquest of Egypt no fresh claim to this dignity is brought forward, in any way connected with the Abbasid Caliph, and if any authorization is suggested, it is made by means of the same verse in the Qur'ān (xxxviii.

* pp. 100–101.

25), that had been quoted by Ottoman Sultans for generations. Thus it occurs in the preamble of the longer account of the Egyptian campaign of 1516–1517, where Salīm is described as ‘ king of the kingdoms of the earth throughout the length and breadth of it, worthy of the allocution “ We have made thee a Khalīfah on the earth ”, auspicious Pādshāh, refuge of the Caliphate, Shadow of God, Sultan Salīm Khān ’.[24] After the same fashion, the Muftī and Qāḍī of Brusa, acknowledging their master’s report of his conquest of Egypt, exhaust all the resources of rhetoric in their letters of congratulation ; the first addresses Salīm as ‘ Your majesty, the Shadow of God, Pādshāh, protector of the world (may his Caliphate last for ever and his empire abide unceasingly by the shield of the help of the Lord !) ’,[25]—and the second, as ‘ Your majesty whose under-garment is the Khilāfat and whose upper-garment is justice . . . (may God firmly establish the pillars of his Sultanate !) ’,[26] and the end of his epistle prays that ‘ the building of this family that bears the stamp of the Khilāfat may be firm as the dome of heaven ’.[27] What is particularly noticeable in the language of these ecclesiastics is that they do not make use of the traditional designations of the Abbasid Caliphs, e. g. Amīr al-Mu’minīn or Imām, nor do they directly address Salīm as Khalīfah ; had they regarded him as the successor of the last Abbasid Caliph they would hardly have refrained from using these titles sanctified by centuries of usage, but the language they use is such as had for generations been applied to Ottoman Sultans before him. Similarly, Salīm himself in his own dispatches quotes, as had been the custom of his fathers before him, the verse 'We have made you Caliphs on the earth' (Qur'ān, vi. 165), when he reports his conquest of Egypt [28] (in a letter to the governor of Gīlān), just as he had done after his defeat of Shāh Ismā'īl in 1514; [29] and in his account of the origin of the Caliphate he ignores the great historic line of the Abbasids and declares that 'the Caliphate was first bestowed upon Prophets and then upon exalted Sultans',[30]—Sultan being a title that any Abbasid Caliph would have scorned to assume.

Strangest of all are the omissions. His son and heir, Sulaymān, in his correspondence with his father uses no title that has any connexion at all with the Caliphate,[31] nor do Shaykh Ibrāhīm, the Shāh of Shīrwān,[32] nor Muẓaffar Shāh II, King of Gujarāt, include it among the many titles they bestow upon Salīm.[33] Similarly, when Sulaymān in 1520 sent letters to the high officials of the empire and to contemporary sovereigns, he (even as his correspondents in their replies) never refers to Salīm as having been a Khalīfah, but only as Sultan, though he might add a string of titles, such as 'my father, the illustrious Sultan, the honoured and esteemed Khāqān, servant of the house of Allāh and of the sanctuary, conqueror of the kingdoms of the Arabs and the non-Arabs' [34] (in a letter to the Amīr of Mecca). Such references in these official documents to the Caliphate are after the same model as those employed by Ottoman Sultans, long before the disappearance of the Abbasid Caliph from Cairo. We miss the earlier titles associated with the reverence of the whole Muslim world, such as Imām or Amīr ul-Mu'minīn ; when Sulaymān does use the latter, he applies it to the Amīr of Mecca, whom he addresses as being 'of the lineage of the Amīr ul-Mu'minīn' (meaning, of course, 'Alī ibn Abī Ṭālib),[35] but never so describes himself, as the great Caliphs of the Abbasid line would have done. A remarkable piece of evidence is provided by an inscription set up in a Madrasa in Cairo, founded in 1543 by Sulaymān's Grand Wazīr, who bore the same name as his master—Sulaymān Pāshā. The Sultan is described as 'the most high Sultan, the exalted Khāqān, lord of the kings of the Arabs and the non-Arabs, breaker of the heads of the Khusraus, subduer of the necks of the Pharaohs, the warrior on the path of God, the fighter for the exaltation of the Word of God, the boast of the Sultans of the Ottoman house, Sultan Sulaymān Khān, son of Sultan Salīm Khān (may God perpetuate his empire and give strength to his power until the rising of the hour and the hour of the uprising !').[36] A Turkish Sultan in those days was not to be trifled with. Sulaymān pitilessly put to death his two eldest sons and his most intimate friend, his Grand Wazīr, Ibrāhīm ; his father is said to have had seven Wazīrs executed. A Prime Minister would never have dared to so describe his master on a public monument, set up in his honour, unless he had been aware of the fact that Sultan Sulaymān attached little importance to the possession of the title of Caliph. Had this title been assumed in Cairo twenty-five years before by means of a transference of it from the last Abbasid Caliph to the Turkish conqueror, here would have been just the occasion for emphasizing the fact of such a succession in the form of a permanent monument, set up in the old seat of the Caliphate.

Little as the Sultan might care for a title that had become so cheap, his flatterers, especially when they were men of letters, were ready to make use of it in their fulsome and long drawn-out panegyrics. One of Salīm's officials, Ibn Zunbul, who accompanied him during his campaign in Egypt and wrote a history of the conquest, gives him the title of 'Khalīfah of God upon Earth'.[37] The historian, Quṭb ud-Dīn, already referred to, who died in 1582 as Muftī of Mecca, described Salīm as 'the most exalted Sultan, the most noble and magnificent Khāqān, the best of the successors of the Caliphs, the most merciful and the most honoured of the descendants of the Sultans of the family of 'Uthmān'.[38]

A similar use of this title was made by the flatterers of later Sultans, e.g. when the Sharīf of Mecca, Barakāt ibn Muḥammad ibn Barakāt, wrote to congratulate Sultan Sulaymān on his succession in 1520, he speaks of ‘ the throne of the most illustrious Sultanate and the seat of the most exalted Khilāfat ’,[39] and prays for ‘ the continuance of the reign of the Khalīfah of God ’.[40] Such appellations are, however, rare in prose, and occur more frequently in poetry, and just as the first appearance of the phrase ‘ Khalīfah of Allah ’ is found in Ḥassān ibn Thābit’s poem on the Khalīfah ‘Uthmān, so the Muftī Abu’s-Su‘ūd, who led the prayers at the funeral of Sultan Sulaymān, wrote an elegy on him, describing him as ‘ axis of the Sultanate of the world and centre thereof, styled Khalīfah of Allah in the far ends of the earth ’.[41] His successor, Salīm II (1566–1574), is described by the same Quṭb ud-Dīn in a poem written in this Sultan’s honour, as ‘ Khalīfah of this age by land and sea ’,[42] and in the account he gives of the re-building of the mosque of the Ḥaram in Mecca, ‘ Khalīfah of God upon His earth ’.[43]

XIII

THE MUGHAL EMPERORS IN INDIA

DURING the sixteenth and seventeenth centuries the only Sunnī monarchs who could rival the Ottoman Sultans in wealth and extent of territory were the Mughal emperors in India. After the manner of their ancestors in Transoxiana, they commonly assumed the title of Khalīfah, and from the reign of Akbar onwards they called their capital *dār ul-khilāfat* (the abode of the Caliphate). Akbar's famous gold coin bore the inscription 'The great Sultān, the exalted Khalīfah'.[1] It certainly never formed any part of the policy of the Mughals to acknowledge the overlordship of the Ottoman Sultan; their own wealth and power made them independent of outside assistance, even if any could have been rendered by an empire so far removed from their own, nor did the current theory of the Caliphate suggest submission to some central Muslim authority. But this attitude of independence did not stand in the way of such complimentary interchange of titles, as has already been noted in the correspondence between Muḥammad I and Shāh Rukh (p. 133), and between Muḥammad II and Ūzūn Ḥasan (p. 135), or Sultan Ḥusayn of Khurasan (p. 118). Correspondence was opened in the name of Akbar in 1557 with Sultan Sulaymān, when Akbar was only a boy of fourteen years of age; advantage was taken of the presence in India of the Turkish admiral, Sīdī 'Alī Kātibī, to establish relations with the Ottoman court, and ' string the kingly pearls of confidence on the thread of affection ' and ' bind together the chains of union and love '. Accordingly, Sulaymān is addressed as ' he who has attained the exalted rank of the Caliphate ', the familiar verse (Qur'ān, xxxv. 37) is quoted, and prayers are offered that his Caliphate may abide for ever. At the same time the Ottoman Sultan is reminded that there is now installed on ' the seat of the Sultanate and the throne of the Khilāfat of the realms of Hind and Sind ', a monarch whose magnificence is equal to that of Solomon.[2]

The same claim was repeated in the reign of Shāh Jahān, when a Turkish ambassador, Arslān Āghā, was dismissed in a rather ungracious manner, after news had reached India of the accession of Sultan Ibrāhīm I in 1640. He was furnished with a letter from Shāh Jahān's minister addressed to the Turkish Grand Wazīr, Muṣṭafà Pāshā; this letter complains that the Mughal emperor, ' his exalted majesty, who occupies the dignity of the Caliphate, the Khāqān of the world, the Shāhinshāh of the Sultans of the whole earth, the Shadow of God ', had not been addressed in language suitable to his high position, and it would appear that at the Turkish court there was no secretary properly acquainted with the etiquette of reat Pādshāhs, and especially of the illustrious house that ruled over India and had ‘thrown the collar of obedience on the necks of all the Sultāns on the surface of the earth’. The writer then goes on to enumerate the various territories under Mughal rule, so vast that travellers marching on every day could not reach to the end of them in the course of a year or even more. Before the letter closes, a word of praise and congratulation is added for the victories of the ‘Khalīfah of the (four) rightly directed Khalīfahs’ (by which unusual appellation was apparently meant the late Sultan Murād IV), who had uplifted the banners of Islam and strengthened the religion of the Prophet.[3] This elicited a courteous reply from the Grand Wazīr, expressing regret for the misunderstanding and a wish for the establishment of friendly relations. But opportunity is taken to emphasize the greatness of the Sultan, on the basis of the very claim that fired the imagination of Salīm I, namely, that in his dominions are comprised the House of God (in Mecca), the grave of the Prophet (in Medina), the holy house (in Jerusalem), and the resting-places of illustrious Apostles and Prophets; and many of the same phrases are employed by the Wazīr to extol his master as were in use two centuries before in the reign of Salīm's grandfather (p. 136), such as ‘the light of the pupil of the eye of the Caliphate, the light of the garden of the Sultanate, . . . the Shadow of God upon earth, the Sultan of the two continents, the Khāqān of the two seas, the servant of the two holy sanctuaries—Sultan Ibrāhīm Khān '.[4]

As the title Khalīfah had been adopted officially by the imperial house, of course historians and men of letters had no hesitation in making use of it, and numerous examples might be given, down to the reign of Shāh 'Ālam II (1759–1806), whose authority for a considerable part of his life was not even effective within the walls of his own palace, yet his biographer lauds him as Khalīfah and Shadow of God.[5]

Nevertheless, in a country like India in which the study of the Traditions was prosecuted with so much zeal, there was always a considerable body of learned men who remained faithful to the earlier doctrine that the Caliphate could belong only to the Quraysh.

XIV

THE LATER OTTOMAN SULTANS AND THE CALIPHATE

THE avoidance of the ancient titles of 'Khalīfah' and 'Amīr ul-Mu'minīn' and 'Imām' in official descriptions of the Ottoman Sultan was possibly due to the fact that the Ḥanafī legists belonging to that school of law which the Ottoman Sultans had taken under their protection, had come to adopt the view (to which reference has already been made) that the Khilāfat had only lasted thirty years, i.e. up to the death of 'Alī, and that afterwards there was only a government by kings. Such was the view of Nasafī (1068–1141),[1] one of the greatest legists of the Ḥanafī school, whose exposition of Muslim doctrine was an accepted text-book in Turkey, and was commented upon by many scholars there. From him this opinion had been adopted by the great Turkish jurist, Ibrāhīm Ḥalabī (*ob.* 1549), whose Multaqa'l-Abḥur became the authoritative Ottoman code of law.[2] It was quite in harmony with such a doctrine that the Turkish 'Ulamā should hesitate to style their ruler 'Khalīfah' or 'Amīr ul-Mu'minīn' in official documents.

Even in the Imperial Chancellery the title Khalīfah seems to have received little consideration, as may be judged from the great collection of diplomatic correspondence, compiled by Aḥmad Firīdūn Bey, secretary to the Grand Wazīr, Muḥammad Sokolli, and presented by him to Sultan Murād III on the feast of Bairām, 1575. To this volume there is prefixed [3] a long list of protocols, setting forth the proper form of address to be employed in documents presented to the sovereign. They are couched in elaborate formulae, made up of a strange mixture of Arabic, Persian, and Turkish, some specimens of which are given in Appendix E. It does not appear that official usage prescribed one single and invariable formula, it being probably left to the epistolary ingenuity of each secretary to elaborate such high-flown eulogies as the occasion inspired. Out of the sixteen alternatives that Aḥmad Firīdūn gives as modes of address to the 'Pādshāh of Islām', there is not a single one that contains the title Khalīfah, and the only reference to the Caliphate is in such phrases as 'janāb-i-khilāfat' (threshold of the Caliphate), 'khilāfat martabat' (who has attained the eminent rank of the Caliphate), 'rauzat-i-khilāfat' (garden of the Caliphate), &c., and these occur only in four out of the sixteen examples given. It would appear that the great-grandson of Sultan Salīm I cared as little for the title that was held to imply the headship of the Muhammadan world as his victorious ancestor had done.

But in the eighteenth century we find this claim beginning to be used for foreign consumption. Turkish diplomats found it convenient to put it forward when dealing with Christian powers, since it implied a relationship between the Ottoman Sultan and Muslims dwelling outside his dominions, that seemed to be analogous to the relationship between Christian powers and members of the same Church living under another government. The first occasion on which such a claim was put forward in a diplomatic document is in the Treaty of Kuchuk Kainarji in 1774. This was a treaty between Sultan Abdul Ḥamīd I and the Empress Catherine II of Russia, in which the Sultan had to recognize the complete independence of the Tartars of the Crimea and of Kuban, countries that had hitherto formed part of the Ottoman empire. The Ottoman plenipotentiaries took advantage of the fact that the Empress of Russia claimed to be the patroness of the Christians of the Orthodox Church dwelling in Ottoman territory, to make a similar claim for the Ottoman Sultan. The Treaty exists in three separate versions—Turkish, Italian, and French—and the language used is not exactly the same in each case. The Turkish version describes the Sultan as: 'The Imām of the believers, and the Khalīfah of those professing the Unity of God.' The Italian version uses the words: 'Supreme Maomettan Caliph.' The French translations give, in one case: 'Grand Caliph of Mahometism,' and in the other: 'Sovereign Caliph of the Mahometan religion.' [4]

The claim to possess religious authority was

made use of, in this treaty, in order to keep a control over the Tartars, who, from that date, were to pass under Russian rule; and the treaty laid it down that in their religious usages these Tartars 'being of the same faith as the Musalmans, must, in regard to his Sultanic Majesty, as Supreme Caliph of the Mahometan law, conform to the regulations which their law prescribes to them, without however in the slightest degree compromising the political and civil liberty which has been guaranteed to them'.[5]

The Turks interpreted this clause as implying that the Sultan would invest the Khan of Tartary, just as in former times the Khalīfah used to send a diploma of investiture to a Muslim prince, and would nominate the officers of the law, Qāḍīs and Muftīs; but the Russians rightly recognized that under this pretended claim of religious authority was concealed an assumption of a political character, and consequently they insisted a few years later (1783) upon having this article struck out of the Treaty.

It is noticeable that the claim made in this Treaty was for the exercise of authority in respect of the organization of what might, from the Muslim point of view, be termed religious organization. The Sultan claimed for himself much the same position as could be claimed in the Orthodox Church by the Empress of Russia, though she possessed no ecclesiastical function. But Western Christendom, ignorant of the relations that subsisted between the head of the Russian State and the Orthodox Eastern Church, invented a comparison which it could much more easily understand, and described the Caliph as holding in the Muslim world much the same position as Catholic Christendom assigns to the Pope.

Such a comparison, indeed, goes back to medieval times. Robertus Monachus, who went on the first Crusade, makes Kerbōghā, the Amīr of Mosil, while he was besieging the Crusaders in Antioch in 1098, instruct his secretary as follows: 'Scribe religioso Papae nostro Caliphae.' [6] But the greater name of Jacques de Vitry, who was bishop of Acre from 1216 to 1226, is probably responsible for the widest extension of this misleading comparison—and how little understanding he had of the Muslim system may be judged from his account of the behaviour of the Caliph. Pope Innocent III had asked for information as to the leading personages among the Saracens, and in the report sent to him, among them were included the sons of Sayf ud-Dīn, brother of Saladin, together with an account of the territories they controlled: the sixth son was stated to be reigning in 'Baudas,* where is the Pope of the Saracens, who is called Kabatus, or Caliphas; who is honoured and revered and according to their law is regarded just as the Bishop of Rome with us;

* i.e. Baghdad, where at that period Nāṣir (1180–1225) was Caliph with more independence than any of his predecessors had enjoyed for several generations.

he can only be seen twice a month when he goes with his people to Machomet, the God of the Saracens. And having bowed the head and prayed according to their law, they eat and drink a sumptuous meal, before they leave the temple, and thus the Caliphas returns crowned to his palace. This God Machomet is visited and revered every day, just as our lord the Pope is visited and revered. In that city of Baudas Machomet is God and the Calyphas is Pope, and this city is head of all the race and law of the Saracens, as Rome is among Christian people'.[7] From Jacques de Vitry, Matthew Paris probably derived his statement that in Baldach (i. e. Baghdad) 'lives the Pope of the Saracens, who is called Caliphus and is feared and venerated according to their law, just as the Roman Pontiff is with us'.[8] Marco Polo, writing about fifty years later, is rather more careful in his language, but he, too, suggests a misleading comparison, when he speaks of Baudas as being a great city, which used to be the seat of the Calif of all the Saracens in the world, just as Rome is the seat of the Pope of all the Christians.[9]

These examples have reference to the historic Caliphate; one more may be given here, drawn from the period when the Abbasid Caliphate in Cairo was drawing to a close; it occurs in an account written by Peter Martyr Anghiera, of an embassy sent to the Mamlūk Sultan, Qānṣūh Ghūrī, by Ferdinand and Isabella of Spain in

1501; the author had been at the taking of Granada by these redoubtable champions of Christendom, and might have been expected to know something of Muslim political theory; but he speaks of the Caliph as follows: 'A summo eorum pontifice Mammetes * confirmatur. Habent enim et ipsi summum pontificem. . . . Is califfas dicitur.' [10]

A similarly erroneous identification was also occasionally made by Muhammadan writers, though with rare exceptions they are singularly incurious as to the details of Christian theory. One of the earliest of these is the great geographer Yāqūt (1179–1229), who speaks of Rome as the city 'in which the Pope lives, who is obeyed by the Franks and occupies with them the position of an Imām; if any opposes him, he is considered by them to be an apostate and a sinner, and must be expelled and banished or put to death'.[11] Another was the historian Sibṭ ibn al-Jawzī (1186–1257), who calls the Pope 'the Khalīfah of the Franks'.[12] A greater name than either of these is that of Ibn Khaldūn (1332–1406); he is more careful in his language, and probably uses the word 'Khalīfah' in its literal meaning as 'successor' without suggesting any analogy between the Christian and the Muslim institution; he explains that each of the Christian sects has its own patriarch, and that of the Melkites is called Pope; the patriarch is considered to be the head

* i.e. the Mamlūk Sultan.

of the church and 'the Khalīfah of the Messiah'.*[13] But his contemporary, Qalqashandī, without hesitation describes the Pope as 'the Khalīfah of the Melkite Christians, to whom they resort for decisions as to what is allowed or forbidden'.[15]

By means of such comparisons, an entirely new characteristic was suggested as being included among the functions of the Caliph, namely, that of spiritual authority, which has a definite meaning in the Christian system, but was altogether inapplicable to the Caliph according to Muslim doctrine. The comparison was popularized in Europe through the influence of M. d'Ohsson's monumental work, *Tableau Général de l'Empire Othoman*, the first volume of which was published in Paris in 1787; in this work he speaks of the 'sacerdotal authority' of the Sultan,[16] and styles him the 'Pontiff of the Musulmans'.[17]

How entirely misleading and incorrect such a comparison is—as false as the account of Islamic doctrine that Jacques de Vitry associates with it in the passage quoted above—may easily be judged by consideration of the fundamental differences between the two faiths, Christianity and Islam.

The Pope is a priest, who, like any other priest, performs the daily miracle of the mass; he can forgive sins, indeed there are certain sins that are reserved for his consideration and he alone can

* This term is also used in modern times to denote the Katholikos of the Armenian Church, or, as an alternative, 'Khalīfah of the Armenians'.[14]

give absolution for them; he can promulgate a new dogma and lay down what is to be believed by the faithful, in virtue of his office as their supreme teacher; he is the final judge in all matters of dispute in reference to religious dogma, and he alone can prescribe the liturgical services employed in the Church; he can canonize saints and grant plenary indulgences; in virtue of his supreme judicial authority certain cases are reserved to him, and he can alter or abrogate the laws made by his predecessors.[18]

Of all these powers there has never been the slightest trace in the Muslim history of the Caliphate, for the Caliph has never at any time been held to be the depository of divine truth. He can promulgate no new religious dogma nor even issue a definition of one. He cannot forgive sins nor exercise any sacerdotal function, nor indeed is there any such thing as a priesthood in Islam. His relation to the Muslim religion is merely that of a protector; as protector of religion he wages war against unbelievers and punishes and suppresses heretics. As leading the prayers during public worship and as pronouncing the Khuṭbah, he can indeed perform definite religious functions, but none of these functions can rightly be described as spiritual. Such spiritual powers as have ever been claimed to exist in the Muslim world have been attributed either to the prophets or to a few of the greatest saints, for some of the prophets and the saints are believed to have performed miracles, and the founders of religious orders could in a mysterious manner communicate spiritual power and confer spiritual blessing; but none of these high privileges have ever been claimed for a Caliph.

In the technical vocabulary of the chief literary languages of the Muhammadan world—Arabic, Persian, Turkish, Urdu—the same distinctions between secular (dunyawī, dunyāwī), religious (dīnī), and spiritual (rūḥī, rūḥānī) are current as in European languages. As in Christian literature, so in Islamic literature, the word spirit (rūḥ) is used in two distinct references: (i) psychological, for the soul of man, and (ii) religious, as in such phrases as rūḥ ul-qudus ('the Holy Spirit'), and it is only in the second sense that the word could have any application when the spiritual authority of the Caliph is spoken of; but the word rūḥī, or rūḥānī, could not be employed in such a connexion by any Muhammadan writer without incurring the imputation of blasphemy. In European languages the word spiritual and its equivalents, especially the French word 'spirituel', is used in a much greater variety of applications, and has not the same narrowed reference as rūḥī or rūḥānī; further, in Christian literature the word has distinctive associations, and has grown up in connexion with an outlook upon theology and the world, entirely different from those belonging to the main currents of Muslim thought.

Nevertheless, from the end of the eighteenth

century onwards, it has become a common error in Europe that the Caliph is the spiritual head of all Muslims, just as the Pope is the spiritual head of all Catholics; that as Sultan he is temporal ruler over the Ottoman dominions, but as Caliph he is supreme spiritual authority over all Muslims, under whatever temporal government they may dwell; consequently, to interfere with the exercise of his spiritual authority, or to fail to respect his claim in this regard, argues an attitude of religious intolerance. There is reason to believe that this widespread error in Christian Europe has reacted upon opinion in Turkey itself. However this may be, it is certain that during the nineteenth century emphasis was laid on the claim of the Ottoman Sultan to be Khalīfah, such as is without parallel in the preceding centuries of Ottoman rule. Sultan Abdul Ḥamīd II, at the very beginning of his reign, had this claim inserted in the Constitution which he promulgated on the 24th December, 1876: 'Art. 3. The Sublime Ottoman Sultanate, which possesses the Supreme Islamic Caliphate, will appertain to the eldest of the descendants of the house. Art. 4. H.M. the Sultan, as Caliph, is the protector of the Muslim religion.'

Abdul Ḥamīd came to the throne at a period of trouble and disaster for the Turkish empire; insurrection had broken out in the Herzegovina and was soon followed by war with Serbia and Montenegro. In the following year, 1877, Russia also declared war, and despite the vigorous resistance offered by the Turkish armies, the result of the campaign was in every way disastrous to Turkey, and finally Russian troops in 1878 encamped outside the walls of Constantinople. The Treaty of Berlin handed over Bosnia and the Herzegovina to Austria; Roumania, Serbia, and Montenegro obtained complete independence, and Bulgaria became an independent state under Turkish suzerainty. Thus deprived of so large a part of his European dominions, the new Sultan appears to have turned his eyes to Asia in the hope that he might there obtain moral support at least. The whole Muslim world had been profoundly stirred by the encroachment of European powers upon dominions that had at one time belonged to Islam; and the disasters that followed the Russian victory through the Treaty of Berlin were all the more impressive in their effect as coming at a time when education and a wider intellectual outlook were changing the Muhammadan world.

The Sultan endeavoured to turn this wave of sympathy to his own advantage by laying emphasis upon his position as Khalīfah, and sought to obtain recognition for himself outside Turkish borders by sending emissaries to Egypt, Tunis, India, Afghanistan, Java, and China, to impress upon the Muslims of those countries that there was still a Khalīfah in Islam. Had he received active sympathy from his co-religionists dwelling under other governments, his position might have gained a considerable accession of strength, and there is no doubt that realization of the dependent state of a great part of the Muhammadan world, as contrasted with its past glories and independence, stimulated in the minds of many Muslim thinkers a desire for unity among the scattered Muhammadan populations. Turkish journalists tried to persuade others that in response to the summons of the Sultan of Turkey, millions of Muhammadans from all parts of the world would rally to his standard.[19] But the emissaries of Sultan Abdul Ḥamīd were ill-chosen. They were not infrequently ignorant of the language of the country to which they were sent and the success of such efforts as they made appears to have been slight. On the other hand, this propaganda came up against the doctrine accepted as orthodox by the majority of Sunnī theologians, that the Khalīfah must be of the tribe of the Quraysh. Even among the Turkish Sultan's own subjects this opposition to his claim made itself felt, and when about 1890 Abdul Ḥamīd ordered the removal from the chief mosques in Constantinople of the tablets containing extracts from authoritative writings setting forth the qualifications required in the Khalīfah,[20] this proceeding did not prove to be a very persuasive argument, and the large body of the Sunnī 'Ulamā stood aloof. On the other hand, some theologians from other countries were persuaded to visit Constantinople, and there received decorations and pensions in recognition of their subserviency.[21] His efforts received more sympathy in those circles that were ignorant of systematic theology, and felt that the political subordination of any Muslim community to non-Muslim rule was an outrage against their faith. But the greatest opposition came from the liberal political thinkers who in consequence of their study of Western literature, or their residence in Europe, were unwilling to lend their support to an irresponsible and cruel despot such as Sultan Abdul Ḥamīd had shown himself to be. His abolition of the Constitution promulgated at the beginning of his reign in December 1876, had shown that no support could be expected from him for any liberal movement in politics, and the number of persons who had been obliged to go into exile in order to escape the persecution of his innumerable spies or even death at the hands of the autocrat, was so great that it is alleged that when the Constitution was re-established in July 1908 as many as 80,000 of such exiles returned to Constantinople.[22] One of the most active workers in the movement, Sayyid Jamāl ud-Dīn (1839–1896), whose ideal was the unity of all Muslims in all parts of the world into one Islamic empire under the protection of one supreme Caliph, recognized clearly enough how unfit Abdul Ḥamīd was to serve as the rallying point for such an ideal, and he used to say: 'Alas! that this man is mad, otherwise I would secure for him the allegiance of all the nations of Islam; but since his name is great in men's minds, this thing must be done in his name.'[23]

So the attempt to revive the earlier associations connected with the Caliphate were doomed to failure: the tyrannies of Abdul Ḥamīd were so notorious, were associated with so much recent suffering, and had created so much distrust in the minds of liberal politicians, that they recognized that the Sultan himself constituted the most serious hindrance to the establishment of constitutional methods of government. Hence the revolution of 1908 and the deposition of Abdul Ḥamīd in the following year.

But the claim made on behalf of the Caliph that he could exercise spiritual authority over the Muhammadan subjects of other governments, was considered too valuable in dealing with European powers, to be readily abandoned by the new constitutional government. After Austria, in October 1908, annexed Bosnia and Herzegovina, the agreement with the Turkish Government stated that the name of the Sultan should continue to be mentioned as Caliph in the public prayers, and that the Ra'īs ul-'Ulamā, the president of the Muslim Curia that controlled ecclesiastical affairs in Bosnia and Herzegovina, should continue as before to be subordinate to the department of the Shaykh ul-Islām in Constantinople, and should have to receive a diploma of investiture from him.[24] A few years later, the treaty of Lausanne

(1912) which declared the sovereignty of the King of Italy over Libya, also recognized the Caliphate of the Sultan of Turkey, and laid it down that his name should be included in the Khuṭbah, and that the head Qāḍī of Libya should be nominated by the Shaykh ul-Islāmat in Constantinople and his stipend should be paid by the Turkish Government, as being a 'spiritual chief', deriving his authority from the spiritual head of the Muslim faith.[25] The Bulgarian Government, in the treaty of Constantinople (1913), did not concede quite so much, but agreed that the chief Muftī should receive from the Shaykh ul-Islāmat authorization for the performance of his functions, but that he should be elected by the Muftīs of Bulgaria from among their own number, just as the other Muftīs were elected by the Muhammadan electors of Bulgaria; but when such an election had taken place, a diploma must be obtained from the Shaykh ul-Islāmat, before any of these new Muftīs could issue decisions on matters of Muslim law, and such judgements should be submitted to the scrutiny of the Shaykh ul-Islāmat, if the parties interested so demanded. The Caliph thus would continue to exercise his spiritual authority in the autonomous kingdom of Bulgaria, through his department controlling the administration of the Sharī'ah. A similar control was conceded in Greece also, by the treaty of Constantinople (1913), but with certain restrictions, in that the King of Greece would nominate the chief Muftī out of three candidates elected by an electoral body made up of all the Muftīs of Greece, and the subordinate Muftīs would receive from him their authorization under a general license granted him by the Shaykh ul-Islāmat.

But the conviction gradually gained strength that the historical associations of the Caliphate were incompatible with a constitutional government responsible to a National Assembly; the very atmosphere of awe and reverence that surrounded the personage bearing the august name of Khalīfah, to whom unquestioning obedience was due, exposed his ministers to the risk of dismissal at any moment, just as in the preceding reigns of Turkish despots. The history of the Abbasid Caliphate in Egypt had shown that it was possible for a Caliph to exist without a single particle of temporal power, though it is unlikely that Turkish statesmen were influenced by any such historical considerations, for they were more concerned with meeting the immediate needs of the political situation in their own country and were most strongly influenced by constitutional theories which might at any time be wrecked by the will of an autocrat. Accordingly, on 1st November, 1922, the Grand National Assembly declared that the office of the Sultan of Turkey had ceased to exist and that its government had become a republic. Sultan Waḥīd ud-Dīn was deposed, and the National Assembly elected his cousin Abdul Majīd as Khalīfah of all the Muslims.

The new dignitary was shorn of all real authority or concern in the political and administrative affairs of the country; he was invested with the mantle of the Prophet, just as his ancestors had been, but he was deprived of the power of the sword, and unlike them, did not proceed to the mosque of Ayyūb to be girt with the sword of the founder of the Ottoman house. His functions appear to have been mainly ornamental; he was present at the weekly Selamlik and was treated with outward formalities of respect; but it had not become clear what place he was to fill in the life of the Muhammadan world, or even in his own country, before this shadowy dignity too was taken away from him, the Caliphate was abolished altogether, and the last Ottoman holder of this ancient title was sent into exile in March 1924.

Speculation as to the future of this institution is out of place in a book concerned only with its historical development in the past. As a political reality, or as embodying the theories that had lent importance to it in the past, the Caliphate had long been dead, and the Turkish National Assembly had faced the realities of the situation in decreeing its abolition.

The theory implied that there was only one supreme ruler in the Muhammadan world, to whom all the faithful owed obedience. But already in the eleventh century there were eight Muslim potentates who called themselves Caliph: the Abbasid in Baghdad, the Fatimid in Cairo, and six princes of less importance in Spain. As to the number of personages who were styled Khalīfah in the fourteenth and fifteenth centuries, some account has already been given in Chapters IX and XI. Even at the present time there is more than one Sunnī Caliph in existence. In the first place, in the opinion of a large number of Muslims the Ottoman Caliph has not been deprived of his dignity by the vote of the National Assembly. The Sharīf of Morocco is still reverenced by his subjects as the possessor of this dignity, which has belonged to his family since the sixteenth century. In assuming the title of Khalīfah, the King of the Hijaz can put forward a claim which no member of the Ottoman house was ever able to make, namely, that he belongs to the tribe of the Quraysh, and thus satisfies one of the earliest requirements as laid down by Sunnī theologians. But in the Malay Archipelago, too, there are several Muhammadan princes who hold this title, such as the Sultan of Jokyakarta in Java, who is styled Khalīfah of Allāh, as is also the insignificant prince of Sambiliung in the island of Borneo; on the east coast of the same island two petty chiefs in Kutei and Pasir call themselves Khalīfatu'l-Mu' minīn, and the Sultan of Tidore in the Malucca Islands, who used to call himself Khalīfatu-l-Mu'aẓẓam (the vicegerent of the Exalted One), is now known as Khalīfatu-l-Maḥfūz (the vicegerent of the Remembered One)—both of these being designations of Allāh.[26] Lastly, in Benkulen, one of the districts of the island of Sumatra, Khalīfah is a common designation for native chiefs.[27]

Under present conditions there seems no immediate prospect of a political community being established in the Muhammadan world under the headship of one Khalīfah, such as Muslim doctrine requires. Nevertheless, the ideal is still cherished, and is likely to survive as a hope in the hearts of Muslim peoples for many generations to come, for every Muslim regards himself as the citizen of an ideal state, in which the earth is the Lord's and the fullness thereof; this state knits together all his brethren in the faith, under obedience to the Imām-Khalīfah, the successor of the Prophet and the vicegerent of God. The aspiration of Islam is to dominate the world, and make the precepts of the Sharī'ah or sacred law effective in every department of administration and the social life; to this end the missionaries of the faith labour unceasingly, and the Khalīfah ought year by year to wage Jihād against unbelievers until there is no government on the earth, save that of Allāh. Among the ignorant there are many Muhammadans who are under the delusion that this ideal has already attained fruition, and that all the Christian powers are but vassals of the Caliph and only govern by his permission. The learned are better acquainted with the actual facts of the modern world; but immersed in the study of the sacred law and the traditional ordinances of their faith, they continue to discuss the application of them under ideal conditions that have no connexion whatsoever with realities, and they long for the day when they may become authoritative exponents of this law in a purely Muslim state. A growing number of Muhammadans, more fully acquainted with modern conditions and more in touch with the aims and ideals of the present day, still cling to the faith of their childhood and the associations that have become dear to them from the Muslim atmosphere in which they grew up. These men likewise cherish an ideal of some form of political and social organization in which self-realization may become possible for them in some system of civilization that is Muslim in character and expression. They resent the predominance of European rule and the intransigeance of European ideas. Even when the dogmas of their faith have little hold upon them, they are still attracted by the glamour of a distinctively Muslim culture and long to break the chains of an alien civilization. To these men, as much as to the others, this hope remains enshrined in the doctrine of the Caliphate.

APPENDIX A

SHIAH AND KHAWĀRIJ DOCTRINES OF THE CALIPHATE

In the preceding account attention has been almost entirely confined to the Sunnī Caliphate because this has played the most important part in the history of the Muhammadan world and for a longer period and over a much larger extent of territory than is the case with any other branch of the Muslim church, but there have been current in the Muhammadan world many more theories than that of the Sunnīs. Liberty of theological speculation may almost be said to have been sanctified by the Tradition ascribed to the Prophet: 'Difference of opinion in my community is a (manifestation of Divine) mercy', and the abundant sectarian development in the Muhammadan world is further recognized by the Tradition: 'My community will become divided into seventy-three sects.' As with other subjects of interest to the theologian and the legist, this of the Caliphate has been abundantly discussed, and some account may well be given here of such speculations as have found embodiment in any actual system of political organization.

Among these, the Shiah first demands consideration, as there have been a number of independent Shiah states, the rulers of which have claimed descent from one or other of the sons of 'Alī: from Ḥasan, the Banū Ukhayḍir in Mecca and the Yaman (866–960), the Idrīsids of Morocco

(788–922), and the Amīrs of Mecca at least during the Middle Ages: from Ḥusayn, the 'Alids of Tabaristan (863–928), the Fatimids (909–1171) in North Africa, Egypt, and Syria, the Zaydī Imāms in the Yaman (860–1281), and the Safavids of Persia (1502–1736). Besides these, there have been other Shiah dynasties that have made no claim to descent from 'Alī, such as the Hamdānids in Mosil and Aleppo during the tenth century and the present Qajar dynasty in Persia from 1779, and the kingdoms of Bijapur, Golkonda, and Oudh in India.

The Shiah theologians have always laid especial stress on the doctrine of legitimacy, and have confined the Caliphate not merely to the Quraysh but still further to the family of 'Alī. They (with the exception of the Zaydīs) reject the principle of election and maintain that 'Alī was directly nominated by the Prophet as his successor, and that 'Alī's qualifications were inherited by his descendants, who were pre-ordained by God to bear this high office. Shiah theory has been developed in forms still further divorced from actual facts than has been the case with the Sunnī theory, for when there was no living Imām (a title which has received more favour among the Shiahs than that of Khalīfah) on earth, the Imām became credited with supernatural characteristics, and it is correct to say that spiritual powers were claimed for the Shiah Imām such as he entirely lacks in the rival Sunnī theory. The Prophet is said to have directly communicated to 'Alī certain secret knowledge, which was in turn handed on to his son, and thus it passed from generation to generation. According to the Shiah doctrine, therefore, each Imām possesses superhuman qualities which raise him above the level of the rest of mankind, and he guides the faithful with infallible wisdom, and his decisions are absolute and final. According to some of the Shiahs, he owes this superiority to a difference in his substance, for from the creation of Adam a divine light has passed into the substance of one chosen descendant in each generation and has been present in 'Alī and each one of the Imāms among his descendants.

The Shiahs broke up into a large number of sects, into the details of which it is not possible to enter here, but according to the sect of the Twelvers, to which the modern Persians belong, the Imām has been hidden from about the year 873, and from his seclusion, invisible to the eyes of men, he guides the life of the community, and until God is pleased to restore the Imām to the eyes of men, legal authority rests with the Mujtahids, the enlightened exponents of the Sharī'ah. In accordance with this theory, the Shāh of Persia is regarded as being only the guardian of public order and makes no claim to be a Caliph. Thus, in the Supplementary Fundamental Laws, promulgated by the Shāh Muḥammad 'Alī in 1907, article 2 ran as follows: 'At no time must any legal enactment of the Sacred National Consultative Assembly, established by the favour and assistance of His Holiness the Imām of the Age (may God hasten his glad advent), the favour of His Majesty the Shāhinshāh of Islam (may God make his reign abide for ever), the care of the Proofs of Islam (i. e. the mujtahids) (may God multiply the like of them), and the whole people of the Persian nation, be at variance with the sacred principles of Islam.'[1]

The Zaydīs, who at the present time are found chiefly in the Yaman, maintain that the Imām should not only be a descendant of Fāṭimah, the daughter of the Prophet, but that he must be elected, and they accordingly refuse to an Imām the right of appointing his successor. They also admit of the possibility of there being two Imāms at the same time, and hold that circumstances may even justify the passing over for a time of the legitimate Imām and the election of some one who has not legally so good a claim.

Further, there are extremists among the Shiahs who have pushed the doctrine of the spiritual authority of the Imām to such an extent as to look upon 'Alī and his descendants as more or less incarnations of the divinity; but in the political history of the Muslim world such doctrines have rarely found embodiment in any organized political system.

The antithesis of Shiah doctrine is taught by the Khawārij. The Khawārij put forward the very contrary of the Shiah doctrine, and represent the extreme left of Muslim political theory. Instead of confining the office of Caliph or Imām to any one particular family or tribe, they hold that any believer is eligible for this exalted office, even though he be a slave or a non-Arab. They further separate themselves from the majority of Muslim thinkers in holding that the existence of the Imām is not a matter of religious obligation, and that at any particular time the community can fulfil all the obligations imposed upon them by their religion and have an entirely legitimate form of civil administration without any Imām being in existence at all: when, under peculiar circumstances it may be found convenient or necessary to have an Imām, then one may be elected, and if he is found in any way unsatisfactory, or if he does not fulfil the precepts of their stern religious creed, he may be deposed or put to death.

The history of the Khawārij is largely made up of a number of revolutionary movements which caused the Muhammadan government much annoyance and anxiety, and they achieved little success in their attempt to make themselves independent. The most important of their political establishments was in Oman. The first recorded election by them of an Imām in this territory is in the year 751, but he was put to death in 753 when the first Abbasid Caliph sent troops to invade Oman. They elected their second Imām in 791, and rose in revolt against the Abbasids and were practically independent for a century; but in 893 Oman was occupied by Abbasid troops, the Imām was killed, and his head sent to the Caliph. No Imāms were elected between 1154 and 1406. The present dynasty that has its capital in Masqat was founded in 1741 by Aḥmad ibn Sa'īd, who was elected Imām after driving out the Persian invaders;

but after the death of his son, no further Imām was elected, and from that period to the present day the Sultans of Masqat have been called Sayyids. From Oman came a colony of Khawārij who settled in Zanzibar. A small group of Khawārij is also found in North Africa, known as the Abādīs.

In addition to these sects, which have succeeded in playing some part in the political life of the Muhammadan world, there have been various speculative doctrines which have never succeeded in gaining for themselves embodiment in any form of political organization.

APPENDIX B

THE ALLEGED SPIRITUAL POWERS OF THE CALIPH

Some of the greatest authorities on Islam have, from time to time, protested against the use of the phrase ‘ spiritual powers of the Caliph ’, and some examples of such protests are given below, in order to show how unjustifiable this vulgar error is.

‘ A côté du vézir et sur la même ligne, mais suivant un autre ordre d’idées, se place le *cheïkh-ul-islâm,* “ l’ancien de l’islâm ”. On a prétendu à tort qu’il était dans l’ordre spirituel ce qu’est le vézir dans l’ordre politique, le délégué du sultan, en tant que pontife et d’imam, successeur des khalifes. Il n’y a point, à vrai dire, de pouvoir spirituel, de même qu’il n’existe pas de sacerdoce dans l'islam. L'attribution propre, essentielle, unique du mufti, c'est l'interprétation de la loi : attribution considérable là où la loi est tout. Chef de l'uléma, de ce corps à la fois judiciaire et religieux, mais n'étant lui-même ni prêtre ni magistrat, sauf dans quelques cas particuliers, il y a dans sa fonction du garde des sceaux, de l'avocat consultant et du doyen de faculté.' [1]

'I have on several occasions pointed out how incorrect it is to represent the Caliph as a "spiritual ruler", like a kind of Pope; people still do not yet sufficiently realize that originally "sultan" means merely "power, authority" (it already occurs in this sense in a Tradition of the time of Omar and in the Kitāb al-umm of Shāfi'ī); if he who exercises power, the Sultan, in the end leaves the Caliph out in the cold and makes the dignity of the Sultan hereditary in his own house, in a word, establishes a Sultan-dynasty side by side with the Caliph-dynasty, then the fundamental position of the Caliph as leader of the community is not thereby shaken or altered, his functions only are restricted; a comparison may possibly be made with the Mayor of the Palace of the Merovingians; there is perhaps also a parallel in the limitation for a whole century of the power of the Japanese Emperor by the Shoguns; it was possible for the Caliph to be rendered powerless just for the very reason that his power was a temporal (mundane) power; this is not possible in the case of the Pope, because his functions are not temporal (are super-mundane): for he has the power of the keys and the power of dogma. The Caliph has nothing that can be in any way compared with this, and it is difficult to understand how the fable of the spiritual power of the Caliphs can have arisen, and how it could have been constantly extended further by scholars who are otherwise intelligent, though no one is able to say what these spiritual functions actually consist of; for the appointment of judges and the conferring of high-sounding titles can certainly not be considered as such.' [2]

'So we see the mediaeval conception of the State slowly accommodate itself to the altered conditions of the times. This is especially the case in the sphere of the particular internal Islam-policy which finds expression in the antithesis—State-control and non-interference in religion. At first sight this problem seems to be actually no problem at all; indeed, if the Caliph were a Pope, this problem would of course not occur; for then we should have before us a complete hierarchy. But the Caliph is no Pope, rather he is the secular ruler of the ideal community. Beside him stands the Holy Law (sheria or sheriat), as the embodiment of the religious factor which is authoritatively interpreted by the chief Mufti of the Hanafi rite, the Shaikh-ul-Islam. As is well known, besides the executive law of the Kadis there is in Islam the consultative law of the Muftis, which may be compared with the legal opinions given by European jurists, and this has just as little binding force on the judges. Since the fifteenth century the Shaikh-ul-Islamat has grown to be the highest religious government office in Turkey. The Shaikh-ul-Islam takes equal rank with the Grand Vizier and is his deputy. Though independent as interpreter of the law, he is in his position himself an official who may be dismissed. So in this way, so far as individual persons are concerned, the problem of State-control and non-interference in religion is settled.' [3]

'The most difficult point of colonial Islam-policy is obviously the relation of the European state to the international claims of Islam. This claim confronts us most conspicuously in the custom of extolling the Caliph of the time in a special bidding-prayer during the Friday service. Throughout the whole history of Islam, the mention of the name of the Caliph at the end of the sermon was an act of special importance. Whoever was mentioned on this occasion, was considered by the community in the particular country to be the real sovereign, who could only incidentally be prevented by external circumstances from exercising the actual power of government. So long as the sultans received their investiture from a Caliph (who might indeed happen to be entirely dependent upon them), this usage was quite in order. But it is quite another question, what should be the relation of a Christian authority to this problem. Properly speaking, the Christian domination shuts out the mention of the name of a Caliph; for, as already stated, the Caliph is indeed no Pope, no spiritual head, but the real sovereign. Nevertheless many European States for various reasons have tolerated and recognized in their territories a bidding-prayer for a foreign ruler.' [4]

'When in 1258 Baghdad was destroyed by the Mongols and the Abasside Caliphate, dating more than five centuries back, was wiped out, the Mohammedan world was not lifted from its hinges, as would have happened if the Caliphate still had had anything to do with the central government of the Mohammedans. In fact this princely house had already been living three centuries and a half on the faint afterglow of its ephemeral splendour; and if during that time it was not crowded out by one of the very powerful sultans, its very practical insignificance was the main reason for that. So insignificant had these Caliphs in name become that certain European writers sometimes have felt induced to represent them as a kind of religious princes of Islam, who voluntarily or not had transferred their secular power to the many territorial princes in the wide dominion of Islam. To them the total lack of secular authority, coupled with the often-manifested reverence of the Moslim for the Caliphate, appeared unintelligible except on the assumption of a spiritual authority, a sort of Mohammedan papacy. Still, such a thing there never was, and Islam, which knows neither priests nor sacraments, could not have had occasion for it. Here, as elsewhere, the multitude preferred legend to fact; they imagined the successor of the Prophet as still watching over the whole of the Moslim community; as, according to historical tradition, he really did during the first two centuries following the Ḥijrah, and this long after the institution of the Caliphate had disappeared in the political degeneration of Islam. However, they did not imagine him as a Pope, but as a supreme ruler; above all, as the *amīr-al-mu'minīn*, commander of the legions of Islam, which some time would make the whole world bend to its power.' [5]

'Probably without intention, some European statesmen and writers have given a certain support to the Panislamic idea by their consideration, based on an absolute misunderstanding, of the Caliphate as a kind of Mohammedan papacy. Most of all did this conception find adherents in England at the time when that country was still considered to be the protector of the Turk against danger threatened by Russia. It was thought useful to make the British-Indian Moslim believe that the British Government was on terms of intimate friendship with the head of their church. Turkish statesmen made clever use of this error. Of course they could not admit before their European friends the real theory of the Caliphate with its mission of uniting all the faithful under its banner in order to make war on all *kāfirs*. They rejoiced all the more to see that these had formed about that institution a conception which to be sure was false, but for that very reason plausible to non-Mohammedans. They took good care not to correct it, for they were satisfied with being able, before their co-religionists, to point to the fact that even among the great non-Mohammedan powers the claim of the Ottomans to the Caliphate was recognized.' [6]

'In the beginning the Caliphs (as their name indicates) were the 'successors' of Mohammed, namely in the guidance and the government of the community. In proportion as the conquests of Islam were extended and firmly established, the Caliphate developed into a princely dynasty, which ruled over an empire and theoretically made claim to the governance of the whole world. We have already drawn attention to the deep roots this theory has struck in the system of Islam and in the popular notions of its adherents. Even after the political dismemberment, which quickly set in, had reached its furthest point, they still continued to cling to the fiction of the unity, and the Caliphs deprived of all real power remained the symbol of this unity, and at least set themselves with their diplomas to put the seal on whatever had come into existence outside their influence.

'In this fiction, however, the Caliphs kept the *name* of whatever their predecessors had been *in reality*; they were called *rulers* of all the lands occupied by Islam, and *never spiritual chiefs*, whose interference was confined to specifically religious matters. The system had indeed been complete from about the tenth century, and its further application took place, just as before its first development, under the guidance of the learned; no one expected it of the central authority, whether real or fictitious. Neither

Muslim statesmen, scholars, or laymen have ever seen in the Caliph anything else but the lawful leader and ruler of all believers.

'When for centuries the obvious impotency of the later Abbasid Caliphs seemed to have put the arrogant doctrine of the Caliphate to shame, the Turks in the sixteenth century were able to restore to this dignity the unity of name and reality. Strong by the might of their weapons, they compelled the majority of the orthodox Mohammedans to recognize them as Caliphs, and they made men forget the conditions which did not suit them, which the law and public opinion had formerly imposed on the Caliph, such as descent from the Quraish, to mention nothing else. The Muslim world always accustomed to bow before the force of facts in politics still more than in any other sphere, accepted the change without much protest, even in countries that had never come into touch with the Turkish Government. Even in the Far East, to which our Indian Archipelago belongs, the Turkish Sultan, under the name of Rajah Rum or of Sultan Istambul, became the revered hero of the popular legend of the Caliphate, and the idea spread among the Mohammedan learned that the princes of Constantinople were the legal rulers of the world, while the other kings and emperors of the earth must be either his vassals or his enemies.' [7]

'The only central organization that Islam has ever possessed, or still possesses, is of a political kind; it has never known anything that can be compared with the papacy or with general councils. The purely spiritual affairs of Islam have for the last thirteen centuries been dealt with by the learned in the various countries, and they could avail themselves of any part that they chose of the light kindled by their fellows in other lands, but were not bound to anything by any oecumenical representation of all Muslims.' [8]

'Even amongst the Moslem peoples placed under the direct government of European States a tendency prevails to be considered in some way or another subjects of the Sultan-Khalīf. Some scholars explain this phenomenon by the spiritual character which the dignity of Khalīf is supposed to have acquired during the later Abbasids, and retained since that time, until the Ottoman princes combined it again with the temporal dignity of sultan. According to this view the later Abbasids were a sort of Popes of Islām; while the temporal authority, in the central districts as well as in the subordinate kingdoms, was in the hands of various sultans. The Sultans of Constantinople govern, then, under this name, as much territory as the political vicissitudes allow them to govern, i.e. the Turkish Empire; as Khalīfs they are the spiritual heads of the whole Sunnite Islām.

'Though this view, through the ignorance of European statesmen and diplomatists, may have found acceptance even by some of the great Powers, it is nevertheless entirely untrue; unless by "spiritual authority" we are to understand the empty appearance of worldly authority. This appearance was all that the later Abbasids retained after the loss of their temporal power; spiritual authority of any kind they never possessed.

'The spiritual authority in Catholic Islām reposes in the legists, who in this respect are called in a tradition the "heirs of the prophets". Since they could no longer regard the Khalīfs as their leaders, because they walked in worldly ways, they have constituted themselves independently beside and even above them; and the rulers have been obliged to conclude a silent contract with them, each party binding itself to remain within its own limits.' [9] *

'Muḥammad had established at once a religion and a State; as long as he lived, both of them had exactly the same territorial extension. Religious authority was always exercised by himself alone, in his quality of prophet and apostle of God; a quality that in his idea and that of his companions did not admit of delegation of spiritual powers to others, nor of transmission of such powers by inheritance after his death. The series of divine

* That the Khalifate is in no way to be compared with the Papacy, that Islām has never regarded the Khalīf as its spiritual head, I have repeatedly explained since 1882 (in 'Nieuwe Bijdragen tot de kennis van den Islam', in *Bijdr. tot de Taal-, Land- en Volkenkunde van Nederland Indië*, Volgr. 4, Deel vi, in an article, 'De Islam', in *De Gids*, May 1886, in *Questions Diplomatiques et Coloniales*, 5me année, No. 106, &c.). I am pleased to find the same views expressed by Professor M. Hartmann in *Die Welt des Islams*, Bd. i, pp. 147–8.

revelations, namely, the Qur'ān, was definitely closed with Muḥammad; after whom the believers had only to faithfully follow his teachings. Hence in Islam there is no trace of any ecclesiastical hierarchy or of sacerdotal holy orders; there is an entire absence of the idea of Christian sacraments, and of an intermediary between God and the individual believer. To find anything that at all approximates to the spiritual powers of the Catholic, Greek, or Protestant clergy we must go to those late manifestations of Islam, about six centuries after Muḥammad, namely, the religious confraternities, in which only there is a true cure of souls, a true spiritual power, which, however, only concerns the relations between the master and the adept who has voluntarily joined the confraternity after the novitiate, and in no way touches either dogma or ritual.' [10]

'Historically the Caliphs are the successors of Muḥammad in the rule of the whole Muhammadan state, i.e. the entire body of the Muhammadans; it being presupposed that there were no Muhammadan populations under non-Muslim rule—as was, in fact, the case for several centuries. But (an inexplicable fact at first sight for a European) these universal monarchs of Islam, just like all other Muslim sovereigns, while they possessed to an unlimited degree executive power and some judicial power, are entirely lacking in legislative power; because legislation properly so called can only be the divine law itself, the Sharīah, of which the 'ulama, or doctors, are alone the interpreters.

In the religious sphere the only attribute of the Caliph, as of any other Muslim sovereign, is to put forth the power of his secular arm in order to protect the faith against internal and external foes, and to take care that public worship, consisting of common prayer on Fridays, is regularly celebrated.' [11]

'The Caliph is the "prince of the faithful", is the universal monarch of the Musalmans, not the head of the Muhammadan religion; in respect of dogma and ritual he is a simple believer, obliged to observe the traditional doctrine as preserved by the 'ulama. He is a defender of the Muslim faith, an enemy of heresy, just as European emperors, kings, and princes were defenders of the faith and extirpators of heresy in past ages.' [12]

APPENDIX C

POPULAR USES OF THE TERM KHALĪFAH

It is a characteristic outgrowth from the Muslim doctrine of the equality of all believers and of the absolute subjection of man to the Will of God and his nothingness as a mere creature, that even the exalted titles enjoyed by the most powerful Muhammadan potentates are applied to persons of a mean and quite insignificant status in society. As a technical term in the administrative language of Egypt, Khalīfah occurs as early as the first century of the Ḥijrah, to denote the representative of a Pagarchos, or local official of the finance department, each one of whom had his Khalīfah or ἀποκρισιάριος at the capital, through whom payments of the taxes were made.[1] In more modern times the term Khalīfah was commonly applied in Turkish official organization to any junior clerk in a public office ; [2] and it was also used in Turkey to designate an assistant teacher in a school, or even an apprentice in the building trade. The historian of the reign of Muḥammad IV (1648–1687), who was a coffee-maker, bore the name of Muḥammad Khalīfah.[3] In the household of the Emperor Bābur, Khalīfah could be used of a woman—an upper maid-servant.[4] In India the word Khalīfah may even be applied to so insignificant a person as a working tailor, a barber, or the foreman of a firm ; sometimes even to a fencing master or a Muhammadan cook. In a more dignified reference it is a technical term in the language of the Sufis, and the authorized exponent of some of the Muslim religious orders may be styled Khalīfah as being a successor of the founder of the order, though the title is often assumed by unauthorized persons who give themselves out as religious guides.[5]

Similarly, as was pointed out on pages 15, 34, the designation Imām may be applied to any one who stands in front of his co-religionists during the act of public worship, and it is no bar to the performance of this function that the person concerned occupies the meanest station in the social order.

APPENDIX D

THE TITLE SULTAN

THE history of the title ' Sultan ' in the Muhammadan world has not yet been fully worked out. The word itself occurs in the Qur'ān merely in the abstract sense of ' power, authority ', but as early as the end of the first century of the Ḥijrah it was used in the Egyptian Papyri as the common expression for the Governor of the province.[1] So it came to be applied to an official to whom power had been delegated, e.g. in the case of Ja'far b. Yaḥyà (*ob.* 803), the favourite of Hārūn ur-Rashīd, the title ' Sultan ' being bestowed upon him (according to Ibn Khaldūn) [2] to indicate that he had been entrusted with the general administration of the empire. In much the same way it was used of Muwaffaq,[3] the brother of the Caliph Mu'tamid (870–892), who had the practical control of affairs of state, both civil and military, the Caliph being wholly given up to his pleasures. As independent rulers set themselves up in the provinces of the empire, it became common among them to adopt the title Sultan, and in this respect the Saljūqs appear to have set the example, though it is commonly asserted that Maḥmūd of Ghazna (998–1030) was the first Muhammadan potentate of importance to so style himself.[4] Like many other titles, it gained in dignity, by being assumed by great and powerful monarchs, while petty princes contented themselves with the name Malik, Khān, &c. The Egyptians during the Mamlūk period liked to flatter themselves that theirs was the only ruler who had a right to call himself Sultan,[5] and the Mamlūks often styled themselves Sultan of Islām and the Muslims.[6]

APPENDIX E

THE TITLES OF THE OTTOMAN SULTAN

THE following are some specimens of the protocols given by Firīdūn Bey as 'Titles of the Pādshāhs of Islam'.

(i) 'His Majesty, the victorious and successful Sulṭān, the Khāqān aided (by God), whose under-garment is victory, the Pādshāh whose glory is high as heaven, King of Kings who are like stars, crown of the royal head, the shadow of the Provider, culmination of kingship, quintessence of the book of fortune, equinoctial line of justice, perfection of the spring-tide of majesty, sea of benevolence and humanity, mine of the jewels of generosity, source of the memorials of valour, manifestation of the lights of felicity, setter-up of the standards of Islam, writer of justice on the pages of time, Sulṭān of the two continents and of the two seas, Khāqān of the two easts and of the two wests, servant of the two holy sanctuaries, namesake of the Apostle of men and of jinns, Sulṭān Muḥammad Khān (may his exalted threshold for ever be a halting-place for the journeys of the saints, and may his exalted court be free from the impurities of diminution and defect).'

(ii) 'Seated on the throne of the exalted sultanate, clothed in the garments of justice and righteousness, guardian of the frontiers of Islam, horseman of the war of vengeance, nay! the mightiest Sulṭān, and most just and noble Khāqān, opener of the gates of benevolence unto mankind, giver of all kinds of bounty in the west and the east, most pious of Sultans in word and deed, most perfect of Khāqāns in knowledge and virtue (may God Almighty make his governance and kingdom endure, and give glory to his helpers and assistants, even as He has exalted his dignity for ever and always, until God inherit the earth and those that are on it, praised and glorious is He!), his majesty, the abode of the Caliphate,' &c.

(iii) 'Star of the imperial fortune, linked with felicity, majesty high as heaven, having its dwelling in the sky, star of the zenith of highness, exalted full-moon of excellence, the first line of the book of kingship, ringlet of the forehead of the asylum of glory, like Faridun in imperial pomp, with a portico like Khusrau's, with a council like Alexander's, moon of the heaven of mightiness, sun of the place where governance arises, exalted in ruling, wise as Darius, containing the high qualities of Kai Khusrau, repeater of memorials like those of Jamshid, laying the foundation of government, engineer of the ways of equity.'

THE ABOLITION OF THE CALIPHATE AND ITS AFTERMATH

BY SYLVIA G. HAIM

THE late Professor Arnold ends his book on these words: 'A growing number of Muhammadans, more fully acquainted with modern conditions and more in touch with the aims and ideals of the present day, still cling to the faith of their childhood and the associations that have become dear to them from the Muslim atmosphere in which they grew up. These men likewise cherish an ideal of some form of political and social organization in which self-realization may become possible for them in some system of civilization that is Muslim in character and expression. They resent the predominance of European rule and the intransigeance of European ideas. Even when the dogmas of their faith have little hold upon them, they are still attracted by the glamour of a distinctly Muslim culture and long to break the chains of an alien civilization. To these men, as much as to the others, this hope remains enshrined in the doctrine of the Caliphate.' To judge by the various steps and measures taken by the Turkish Grand National Assembly (GNA) in order to abolish the Caliphate, and by the general reaction which followed this abolition in the Islamic world, Professor Arnold was fully justified in making such a statement. He writes that the Ottoman Caliphate was abolished and the Caliph sent into exile in 1924.[1] This simple statement does not fully convey the complexity of the events; on the contrary, the abolition had to be carried out in two stages and, naturally, did not pass undiscussed in the Muslim world. The law of 1924 which finally dissolved this venerable institution was being prepared for both inside and outside Turkey by the Turkish press, and was foreshadowed by the law of November 1922—which, strangely enough, was received rather quietly by all those concerned with the Caliphate.

In Chapter XIV Professor Arnold explains clearly how the Ottoman Sultans slowly began to exploit the idea of the Caliph as the Pope of Islam which they derived from European sources, how, from the eighteenth century onwards, they arrogated to themselves, in their dealings with Europe, the title of Caliph, and how, through mistaken comparison with the Papacy, a new characteristic, that of spiritual authority, began to attach itself to the idea of the Caliphate. Therefore as Professor Arnold points out, 'from the end of the eighteenth century onwards, it has become a common error in Europe that the Caliph is the spiritual head of all Muslims, just as the Pope is the spiritual head of all Catholics; that as Sultan he is temporal ruler over the Ottoman dominions, but as Caliph he is the supreme spiritual authority over all the Muslims, under whatever temporal government they may dwell'.[2] It is unnecessary to repeat what Professor Arnold explains so well: how this European misconception was taken over by Ottoman Turkey, with what shrewdness Sultan Abdul Hamīd exploited it in the Constitution of 1876 and throughout his reign until he was deposed in 1909. The new Constitutional government found it useful and expedient in its relations with Europe to develop the conception of the spiritual power of the Caliph. The declaration of Jihād, Holy War, in 1914 however had very little concrete significance, and not even the Indian Muslims—who later on were to show the greatest devotion and loyalty to the Ottoman Caliph—were to fight on his side. The defeat of Turkey in the War and the advent of Muṣṭafà Kamāl made the new leaders of Turkey turn their backs on the Caliphate and concentrate their efforts into building a new and modern nation. It is in this light that the National Pact of January 28, 1920 is to be understood. It renounced all claims to dominion over 'portions of the Ottoman Empire inhabited by an Arab majority', i.e. including the Holy cities of Islam the guardianship of which was a prerogative of the Caliph, this in spite of the fact that it confirmed that 'the security of the city of Constantinople, which is the seat of the Caliphate of Islam, the capital of the Sultanate and the head-quarters of the Ottoman Government . . . must be protected from every danger'.

The Sultan-Caliph Muḥammad VI Waḥīd ud-Dīn who had come to the throne in July 1918 and whom the Armistice of October 30, 1918, freed from the control of the Committee of Union and Progress, threw in his lot against Muṣṭafà Kamāl and the Nationalists and, responding a little no doubt to the pressure of the Allies, issued a Fatwā on April 5, 1920, to the effect that the behaviour of the Nationalists was contrary to Islam.[3] A counter Fatwā by Muṣṭafà Kamāl did not leave the matter at rest and more blows had to be administered to the power of the Sultan-Caliph in order that the new provisional government, which on April 25, 1920, elected Muṣṭafà Kamāl President of the Assembly and effectively took over the administration of the country, should gain full control of the situation. The first step in the abolition of the Caliphate was taken by the GNA when they voted the law of November 1922; this law abolished the Sultanate in favour of the government of the Turkish GNA as from March 1920, the date on which the Allies had occupied Constantinople.[4] Having won his victories over the Greeks in Thrace in October 1922, Mustafà Kamāl was strong enough to make the necessary constitutional changes. This law in fact followed logically on previous announcements. Mustafà Kamāl had said in his motion of April 24, 1920, to the GNA, referring to the formation of the new government, that the Sultan would have to decide his position within the legal framework which the Assembly would determine, when he became a free agent again. Moreover the Constitution accepted by the Assembly on January 20, 1921, had already declared that 'Sovereignty belongs unconditionally to the people. The administration derives from the principle that the people control their destiny in person and in fact.'[5]

The law of November 1922 also decreed that the Caliphate resided in the Ottoman dynasty and that the member of the dynasty best qualified in character and knowledge was to be elected Caliph by the GNA. The administration of Constantinople was taken over and the Ottoman Government ceased to exist. The ex-Sultan-Caliph took refuge on board a British battleship; he then proceeded to Malta then to Mecca as guest of King Ḥusayn. A Fatwā was rendered to the effect that Wahīd ud-Dīn Effendi had forfeited the office of the Caliph, and a declaration of allegiance (Bay'ā) to some other person was necessary. On November 18, 1922, the GNA voted unanimously that this Fatwā rendered the office of the Caliphate vacant without further action on their part, and they immediately elected Caliph Abdul Majīd Effendi, the second son of Sultan Abdul 'Azīz, who had been deposed in 1876. There were limitations however not only on the powers of the Caliph but also on Abdul Majīd's freedom even in connexion with the caliphal regalia.[6] It will be recalled that the Ottoman Government had emphasized in the nineteenth century the spiritual authority of the

Caliph over the Muslims outside the Ottoman Empire. Is it not legitimate to wonder whether this final step separating the so-called spiritual from the so-called temporal power of the Caliph was not the logical conclusion of that line of argument, and whether in fact the fallacious doctrine adopted as a convenience by Sultan Abdul Ḥamīd did not in the end boomerang on the Ottoman dynasty.

This law of 1922 which limited the power of the Caliph by taking away his temporal authority was not the only preparation for the later law of 1924 abolishing the Caliphate altogether. Canonical arguments were also exploited. At the end of 1922 the GNA put out a semi-official unsigned document which had been prepared by a group of 'Ulama under the direction of a member of parliament in order to prepare Muslim public opinion both inside and outside Turkey for the complete absorption of the Caliphate into the nation. This document is decisive because it expressed the canonical arguments on which the Republicans based their abolition of the Caliphate. A complete and authorized translation of the document into Arabic was made by Abdul Ghani Sani, Turkish Consul in Beirut and official spokesman for the GNA, and published in *al-Ahrām* in 1924. The translation was prefaced by an article which Abdul Ghani Sani had originally published in *al-Ahrām* on November 14, 1923.[7] In this preface he argues that the question of the Caliphate is not a matter of theology but one of law. Sunni jurists, he points out, have found it necessary to devote long discussions to this question in order to refute the many false notions which have adhered to it. They speak in this connexion of the Caliphate without mention of the Imamate in order to emphasize that the question of the Caliphate in its essence is absolutely secondary, that it is in the field of law and that it must be considered purely as a political and temporal matter to be treated directly by the Muslims.[8] Moreover, claims Abdul Ghani Sani, there is no precise indication in the Qur'ān or the Ḥadīth relating to the basic questions of the Caliphate. It is to be noted that Muḥammad who devoted, for instance, so much attention to the question of hygiene leaves this question undiscussed in the Qur'ān. There is indeed in the Qur'ān general advice that obedience is due to the holder of power, but it is only logical to conclude that the Caliphate is not a fundamental requirement of Islam for how otherwise could it be stated, he asks, that ' Islam is completed in Muhammad's lifetime '. It is therefore obvious that Muḥammad named no successor and gave no advice about the Caliph in order to leave to the Muslims the freedom to deal with this question because it is more temporal than religious. In fact, says Abdul Ghani Sani, the majority of competent Sunnis deny certain claims made by 'Ulamā, Shi'ite as well as some Sunni, that Muḥammad had nominated either 'Alī or Abu Bakr to be his successor. If this has been the case, how then to explain so much dissension after his death? It is obvious from this preface what the drift of the argument will be.

The argument of this document is intricate, at times contradictory, always tortuous, and often difficult to keep in check. The conclusions are quite easy to grasp and the authors use any convenient, expedient and tactical device to reach their conclusions even though at times they may contradict themselves. They argue that the Caliphate is not a religious requirement but only an ancient custom, they explain how the Sultanate had been separate from the Caliphate for centuries, and how the power of the Caliphate had always been restricted thanks to the system of deliberation and other means. The document itself is divided into two parts, the first of which deals with the legal and historical background of the Caliphate and the second with the question of separation of powers and with the restriction of the powers of the Caliph. The arguments used intermingle and it is not always easy to distinguish between them. Intellectual somersaults are necessary in order to follow the line of argument which, at the start, claims that the power of the Caliph has nothing spiritual about it, and which ends by abolishing the Sultanate, i.e. the temporal power and yet still claims to retain a spiritual Caliphate. These ambiguities and contradictions may of course indicate that even in 1922 Muṣṭafà Kamāl had in mind the ultimate abolition of the Caliphate, and this is in fact what he himself claims to have been the case.

In the first part of the document the authors argue that Islam is sublime : no hierarchy and no spiritual authority attaches to any of its members, be he Caliph, Muftī or Shaykh ul-Islam ; the laws of Muslim jurisprudence are not divine prescriptions but authoritative pronouncements made by learned Muftīs. If any man is not convinced by a particular Fatwā it is open to him to request as many opinions as he can obtain until he is satisfied. The Caliph, otherwise Imām, is the head of the Muslim community : the full and complete power which he holds however is not like that of the Pope, inherently spiritual, but resembles rather the authority of the President of a Republic, or of an administrative and political ruler or head of state. A distinction is made here between the real and the fictitious Caliphate. The real Caliphate, the authors claim, is based on free choice, on the acceptance and the solemn acclamation of the whole nation. This Caliphate follows the guidance of the Prophet in its exemplary behaviour, its noble character and in the administration of the political and religious affairs of Islam. In its relation to the nation, it is called the Caliphate of the Nation, and it has a mandate over the nation. It is subordinate to the choice, the complete adherence and the solemn recognition of the nation. It is very important for the authors to repeat again and again that the only real Caliphate has been that of the Rashidūn and that the Abbasid and the Umayyad have been fictitious which means that, although they appeared in the same guise and the same setting, they only had the outward show of the real one; fictitious Caliphates only establish despotism and arbitrariness. The next point of the argument is the distinction between the true or real Caliphate where justice obtains and the Sultanate which is not based on the free choice of the people but on despotism. We may well ask here, the document says, whether the Sultanate is the same as the fictitious Caliphate; it is at times extremely difficult to distinguish one from the other. It is essential to understand the distinction between the real and the fictitious Caliphate in order to understand whether it is legal to separate the Caliphate from the Sultanate. The qualifications for election as Caliph are numerous and well-known—although Qurayshi descent as a necessity has long fallen into disuse—and unless it is possible to elect a Caliph with all these qualifications there is no religious obligation to elect one at all. This, however, does not mean that the Muslims have to dispense with a government. Moreover the possession of the necessary qualifications alone cannot make a person into a Caliph; no man can arrogate to himself the power of the Caliph; he has to be invested by the nation. The question of the Caliphate as a mandate is gone into more fully. The jurists, so the document claims, say that the Caliphate is a kind of mandate entrusted by the nation to the Caliph, that it is a contract offered by the nation, concluded and accepted by both parties. Just as no man can exercise a mandate without being given the power, in the same way no one can, on his own initiative and without being invested by the nation, fulfil the function of the Caliphate. A man can only become Caliph when the people, having judged him worthy of fulfilling these duties, willingly offer him this function. He must also (willingly)? accept this offer and promise to fulfil this mission. The Caliphate then is only the contract involved in such a situation and it is no different from a power of attorney. All the rules of mandate must apply and the Caliph can be deposed by the nation.

The document equates the Bay'ā of Ahl al-Ḥall wa'l-'Aqd with the power of attorney given by the whole nation; it represents the Caliphate as a form of democratic rule obtained by plebiscite. This is very far removed from the orthodox conception and is only reached by an extension and a perversion of the traditional official view of Bay'ā and Ahl al-Ḥall wa'l-'Aqd.[9] The authority and the power called al-Wilāya al-'Ammā which the Caliph holds over the nation are fully detailed; they are the rights inherent in the people and it is from the people that the Caliph acquires them. The people invest the Caliph with this authority in the same way that any man may entrust to a guardian through a power of attorney the administration of his own affairs. Religion only affirms this duty. There is therefore no difference in law between a Caliph and a guardian. The authority that the Caliph exercises therefore belongs in fact to the Muslim community and no one can take it over, yet everyone has a share in it. It is a whole belonging in common to all Muslims.

The Caliphate is not an end in itself but a means to an end; it is no more than a form of government instituted to secure the happiness of the Muslims, to administer justice, to protect the rights of the people and in this way to fulfil the principal aims of Islam. It is therefore obvious that the power held by the Sultans and the Padishahs is illegal and that obedience to them was not voluntary but necessary and submission compulsory. In such cases it is a duty to disobey if possible and even to depose the Caliph if this does not lead to worse conditions.

In the second part which deals with the separation of the Sultanate from the Caliphate and with the restriction of the power of the Caliph, the authors, having established that the function of the Imamate is to have a just and regular government, ask the question: Is it necessary to have an Imām with general authority over the Muslims when it is possible to obtain a just and regular government under another form? Or in other words, the foundation of a regular and just government being possible, does the obligation to nominate an Imām holding absolute power still impose itself? The argument in favour of the separation of the Sultanate from the Caliphate is a complex one. Religion imposes restraints on the power of the Caliph : consultation, Shūra, is one of the fundamental principles of Islam, and the mandate given by the nation to the Caliph is a form of restraint because it is the people who impose the conditions upon which this power is held and it is up to them to cancel this mandate if they find it necessary. The Caliph himself moreover delegates duties and rights to one person or to many or to the members of an executive council or to a national assembly or to the whole of this governmental organ. This in fact is what happened in Egypt for at least 250 years when Caliphs delegated their functions to Sultans. It is quite clear that during all this time the Caliphate was not a religious duty but merely an ancient custom and a mark of honour and distinction. Another line of argument is the following : After the Rashidūn the Caliphate has been despotic and contrary to the principles of religion and of the Prophet ; people are forced through necessity to obey it, fearing worse conditions ; otherwise they would have been duty-bound to depose the Caliph. In the case of Caliph Waḥīd ud-Dīn, there is no more point in acquiescing in despotism because this Caliphate does not achieve any of the aims for which it exists ; that is why the people, represented by the GNA, must take over. In conclusion, the document states that it is quite clear then that Islam did not prescribe a particular governmental system, but only that justice and order should prevail. It is therefore immaterial how this is attained.

This document which argues for the abolition of the Sultanate seems to point quite clearly to the next step, the abolition of the Caliphate which had been declared spiritual in 1922. The most interesting evidence showing how early these various steps were planned comes from Muṣṭafà Kamāl himself in a speech which he gave as President of the Republic in October 1927. In this speech which lasted from the 15th to the 20th October Muṣṭafà Kamāl gave a comprehensive account of his actions from the time he landed at Samsun on May 19, 1919. It is interesting to read what he says about his own solution of the problem of the Caliphate. He claimed that from the start he saw quite clearly that

> to labour for the maintenance of the Ottoman dynasty and its sovereign would have been to inflict the greatest injustice upon the Turkish nation; for, if its independence could have been secured at the price of every possible sacrifice, it could not have been regarded as secure as long as the Sultanate existed. How could it be admitted that a crowd of madmen, united by neither a moral nor a spiritual bond to the country or the nation as a whole, could still be trusted to protect the independence and the dignity of the nation and the State?

> As for the Caliphate, it could only have been a laughing-stock in the eyes of the really civilized and cultured people of the world.

Starting from such a view, he had to decide upon a line of action and in this he was governed by the way of thinking of the nation which he had to bring up to his own level.

> As you see [he says], in order to carry out our resolution, questions had to be dealt with about which the nation had hitherto known practically nothing. It was imperative that questions should be brought forward that could not be discussed in public without giving rise to serious dissensions.
>
> We were compelled [he goes on to say], to rebel against the Ottoman Government, against the Padishah, against the Caliph of all the Mohammedans, and we had to bring the whole nation and the army into a state of rebellion.
>
> It was important [he emphasizes], that the entire nation should take up arms against those who would venture to attack the principal part of Turkey and its independence, whomsoever they might be. It would undoubtedly have been of little advantage if we would have put forward our demands at the very beginning in a resolution of such far-reaching importance. On the contrary, it was necessary to proceed by stages, to prepare the feeling and the spirit of the nation and to try to reach our aims by degrees,

profiting meanwhile by our experience. This is actually what happened.

If our attitude and our actions during nine years are examined in their logical sequence, it is evident from the very first day that our general behaviour has never deviated from the line laid down in our original resolution, nor from the purpose we had set out to achieve.

In order to dispel any doubts which might still be entertained, one fact is urged upon us for mutual examination. As the national struggle carried on for the sole purpose of delivering the country from foreign invasion, developed and was crowned with success, it was natural and inevitable that it would gradually, step by step to the present day, have established all the principles and forms of government founded on national sovereignty. The sovereign of the dynasty who, thanks to his traditional instincts, foresaw this fatal course of historical events, declared himself from the very beginning the most embittered enemy of the national struggle. I, also, from the first could see what would be the result. But we never disclosed the views we held. If we had done so we would have been looked upon as dreamers and illusionists. If we had offered explanations we might from the outset have alienated those who, discouraged by the possibilities arising from dangers threatened from abroad, were fearful of eventual revolutionary changes which would be contrary to their tradition, their way of thinking and their psychology. The only practical and safe road to success lay in making each step perfectly understood at the right time. This was the way to ensure the development and restoration of the nation.

This was how I acted [he explains even more]. This practical and safe way, however, as may easily be understood, provoked certain differences of opinion of more or less importance, and even the discouragement and dissension which was observable from time to time between us and our most intimate co-workers; differences of opinion, sometimes in regard to principles, at others as to the method of the execution of our programme. Some of my companions who had entered into the national fight with me went over to the opposition, according as the limitation of their own mental appreciation led them and their moral courage succumbed in the effort to develop national life, to proclaim the Republic and enact its laws. I shall refer to these cases individually as I proceed in my statement.

To summarize what I have been saying, I may add that it was incumbent upon me to develop our entire social organization, step by step, until it corresponded to the great capability of progress which I perceived in the soul and in the future of the nation and which I kept to myself and in my own consciousness as a national secret.[10]

The clarity and precision with which this policy is subsequently presented do not necessarily reflect such decisiveness when action was being taken; Muṣṭafà Kamāl's successive moves must have been cautiously planned, and the pattern which in 1927 he imposes on his thoughts and actions must have become visible to him only in retrospect. The three laws which finally destroyed the religious order were passed at the beginning of March 1924: they dealt with the abolition of the Commissariat for the Awqāf, with the unification of the educational system and with the abolition of the Caliphate.[11] 'With regard to myself', Muṣṭafà Kamāl amplifies, 'I was of the opinion that after the abolition of the monarchy, the caliphate, being only an authority of a similar description under another name, was also abolished. I found it quite natural to express this opinion at a favourable moment. It cannot be maintained that Abdul Mejid who was elected Caliph', he goes on to say in a most interesting observation, 'was quite ignorant of this fact.'[12] Some time earlier Abdul Majīd did in fact express in a communiqué to the press a certain discomfort because his 'religious' duties were not clearly defined. The separation of the spiritual from the temporal power of the Caliph had created such an absurd situation that the logical step must have been quite obvious to anyone willing to see.[13] This situation was made even more vague by the law of October 29, 1923, which not only reaffirmed that sovereignty belonged absolutely and unconditionally to the nation but also proclaimed Turkey a republic, stated that the religion of the state was Islam and that the chief of the state was the President of the Republic.[14] A man with a tremendous sense of reality and a clear vision as he appears to be,[15] Muṣṭafà Kamāl again explains in a letter of January 1924 that the Caliph must compare his own position *vis-à-vis* the community with that of the British Monarch *vis-à-vis* the Muhammadan population of India, or of the Government of Afghanistan *vis-à-vis* the people of Afghanistan. 'The Caliph himself and the whole Muslim world must know in a categoric manner that the Caliphate and the office of the Caliph as are now maintained and exist, have in reality neither a material nor a political meaning nor any right of existence.'[16] Moreover the cost of the Caliphate to Turkey more than irritated him.[17] It was natural then for such a man to decline the title for himself when it was tentatively offered to him—as he claims—on behalf of the Muslims of India and of Egypt, in these words :

> You know that Caliph signifies Chief of the State. How can I accept the proposals and desires of people who are governed by kings and emperors? If I should declare myself to accept this office, would the sovereigns of these people consent to it ? The orders of the Caliph must be obeyed and his interdictions submitted to. Are those who want to make me Caliph in a

> position to execute my orders? Consequently, would it not be ridiculous to rig me with an illusionary rôle which has neither sense nor right of existence? [18]

In his *Speech* Muṣṭafà Kamāl argues as though he had seen from the outset the necessity of abolishing the Caliphate;[19] but a public utterance three years after the event is not conclusive evidence of the existence of a deliberate, gradually unfolding plan. We may suspect that in reality confusion and improvisation were the order of the day, and that it is only hindsight which supplies the neat predictable sequence.

The incompatibility between the Caliphate and the Republican Government was such[20] that Abdul Majīd, in spite of his co-operation with the régime and because his person proved a rallying point for the opposition,[21] was expelled and on March 4, left for Switzerland together with his family. His call for a congress to solve the problem only served to anger the Swiss authorities who had given him refuge. This move on the part of the Ankara Government created intellectual confusion in the Muslim world, especially among the Indian Muslims, and the only practical step to which the subsequent discussions and agitations led was the Congress for the Caliphate which met in Cairo in 1926 but which was only partially attended by some Muslim delegates.

On March 5, King Ḥusayn of the Ḥijāz who had

declared himself King in 1916, accepted in Transjordan the oath of allegiance, Bay'ā, to him as Caliph.[22] This act which was quickly followed by his defeat at the hands of the Wahhābis and his abdication from both the Caliphate and the kingship was considered a mockery by the largest section of Islam. Propaganda in his favour was based mainly on the claim he could make to Qurayshi descent, one of the fundamental qualifications for the Caliphate. Professor Arnold explains how, very early on in the history of Islam, this clause fell into abeyance, and yet it is the one clause about which there is hardly any disagreement among the Sunnis.[23] It is interesting to note that some Arab writers and thinkers have been trying from the beginning of the century to revive the idea of an Arabian Caliphate in favour of a Qurayshi candidate in spite of the fact that this qualification was not in itself sufficient for claiming the office. The earliest discussion on these lines made in Arabic was by 'Abd ur-Raḥmān al-Kawākibī (1849–1902) in his book *Umm al-Qura* where he describes an imaginary meeting of delegates from all the Muslim communities in Mecca.[24] He concludes that the problem of Islam, its weakness, its decadence, its inability to compete with the civilized nations, etc. . . . are to be solved by having an Arab Caliph from Quraysh to be installed at Mecca, whose political authority will extend over the Ḥijāz only and will be exercised with the concurrence of a special Council of

Consultation, Shūra. The functions of this Caliph would be very restricted and he could not interfere in the political or administrative affairs of the Muslim Amirates and Sultanates beyond giving his approval to the appointment of Sultans and Amīrs. He is to have no army and his name is to be mentioned in the Khuṭbah before the names of the Sultans but it is not to be minted on coins. He seems to be the figure-head *par excellence*, completely devoid of any real power, and yet necessary for the creation of an Islamic Union. He is to be elected according to special rules and regulations, and generally his election is to be renewed every three years.[25]

This choice of a Caliph from Quraysh is not haphazard, on the other hand it is not based merely on the religious needs of such a function. In al-Kawākibī's scheme, a scheme which is principally anti-Ottoman and pan-Arab, the choice of the Caliph is based on what he claims to be a deep study of the situation of the Muslim peoples. This study has led him to the belief which he claims is based on the historical fact that the Peninsula Arabs, because of their central position in Islam, because of their language which is that of revelation, because of the purity of race, belief and practice prevalent among them, because of their beduin characteristics of pride, their ability to bear hardships, their adaptability to changing conditions, their possession of the Holy Places, their antiquity and their love for independence and freedom, because of their poverty which would protect them from the greed and the cupidity of other nations, are the best suited to carry out the function of the Caliphate, one of the many functions necessary for the running of this Islamic Union. These functions are to be shared out among all the Islamic peoples each according to his best abilities, i.e. diplomacy for the Ottomans, administration for the Egyptians, the organization of military forces to the Afghans and their neighbours in the East and to the Moors in the West—Persia, Central Asia and India to take care of culture and economics. It is quite obvious from this summary that al-Kawākibī's conclusions in favour of a Qurayshi Caliph were not made on the religious premise of the necessity of descent from the Prophet but rather from sociological premises. His possible debt in these most unorthodox plans to W. S. Blunt (1840–1922), an English man of letters who was widely travelled in the Levant, Arabia, India, and long resident in Egypt, has been studied in a detailed fashion. Blunt like al-Kawākibī represents the Ottomans not as the upholders but as the corrupters of Islam; this point of view has been amply developed by the Arab historiographers of the past half century. It is interesting to quote here Blunt's opinions of the benefits to Islam that an Arabian Caliphate would have.

> One great result the fall of Constantinople certainly will have, which I believe will be a

> beneficial one. It will give Mohammedanism a more distinctly religious character than it has for many years possessed and by forcing believers to depend upon spiritual instead of temporal arms will restore to them, more than any political victories would do, their lost moral life. . . . The fall of the Mussulman Empire [he continues], as a great temporal dominion, would relieve Islam of a burden of sovereignty which she is no longer able in the face of the modern world to support. . . . The Caliph of the future [he explains], in whatever city he may fix his abode, will be chiefly a spiritual and not a temporal king.

Blunt wrote in 1881 but the idea of a spiritual Caliphate so clearly mooted by him did not appear in a Muslim source, as has been seen, until twenty years later. Immediately after al-Kawākibī, who it has been suggested may have been an agent of the Khedive Abbas Ḥilmi or of the Italians,[26] Negib Azoury, a Syrian Catholic whom it is difficult to believe not to have been in the pay of the French found in 1905 in Paris *Le Parti National Arabe de la Turquie* which brought out a manifesto in the name of the *Ligue de la Patrie Arabe.* Azoury commends this manifesto for the benefits it will give : the temporal and the religious powers are to be separated in the interests of both Islam and the Arab nation.[27]

Views like these it may seem would have prepared the field for the election of Ḥusayn as Caliph, but his short-lived Caliphate was only recognized in a very limited manner and met with great indignation from the largest sections of Islam, especially from Egypt and India.[28] It is interesting to note that Rashīd Riḍā, that most prolific of writers and greatest of publicists for the pan-Arab cause, a man who always wrote with integrity about the necessity of Qurayshi descent, was aroused to such a pitch of indignation at this move on the part of Ḥusayn that he wrote of this despot, Ṭāghut, of the Ḥijāz who had falsely claimed to exercise kingship over all the Arabs and the Caliphate over all the Muslims and whose designs God had defeated by stripping him of his alleged authority, and leaving him cut off from the community, abandoned, and hated and execrated.[29] Rashīd Riḍā in *al-Khilāfa wa 'l-Imāma al-'Uẓma* which he wrote in 1922 immediately after the abolition of the Sultanate by the GNA discusses fully the question of the Caliphate. This problem had always interested him and in his review *al-Manār* which the Ottoman authorities banned in their territories very early on, he was always in favour of autonomy for the Arabs within the Ottoman Empire and of transforming the Ottoman Caliphate into a central organ for religious apostolate rather than turning it into a tool for political panislamism.

He hoped to start in Constantinople a college for Islamic propaganda and guidance, a hope which materialized in a much smaller college in Cairo supported financially by a few wealthy Indians and by the Khedive Abbas and which had to shut down as soon as the War started. He was disappointed in the Hamidian régime in spite of the sympathies he expressed for it, and he felt that it could hardly serve towards a reform of Islam or towards conciliating the newly rising Turkish and Arab nationalisms. The growth of Turkish secularism and the abolition of the temporal power of the Caliphate and then of the Caliphate altogether led Rashīd Riḍā to this now topical issue.[30] In the first part of his study he gives the orthodox Sunni view of the Caliphate. He expects his Caliph to have all the necessary moral, physical and technical qualities, to possess the power of Ijtihād as well as to be of Qurayshi descent. This question of descent has always created perplexity and it may be of interest to mention in passing that when King Fāruq hoped to gain the title for himself he had the Naqīb al-Ashrāf of Egypt, whose principal function is to maintain a record of the genealogy of the descendants of the Prophet, provide a family tree for him going back to Muhammad.[31] The Caliph, in the opinion of Rashīd Riḍā, is to be both the spiritual and temporal leader of his subjects, to be responsible for the protection of religion as well as to administer the material interests of the community. In the second half of his study, Rashīd Riḍā naturally runs into difficulties in trying to apply those requirements to the conditions of the time. He goes carefully over all the possible candidates in all the Muslim countries. Ḥusayn he scorns for his love of power, incompetence in canonical matters, and above all his subservience to Britain. Turkey he respects for her military ability but he is more than doubtful of her secularist tendencies ; about the possible Egyptian candidate he remains silent. His sympathies are with the Wahhābis yet as a person it is the Imām Yaḥya of the Yaman whom he considers because of his Qurayshi descent, his learning and his semi-independence, the most suitable candidate. He sees nevertheless the impossibility of solving this problem immediately and practically and he reverts once again to his original idea of a college.

The best examination perhaps of all the possible candidates is to be found in a letter to Rashīd Riḍā from Shakīb Arslān written on May 12, 1924 after the abolition of the Caliphate.

> You object to the purely Spiritual Caliphate [writes Shakīb Arslān], that invention that some people have invented for well-known reasons, and which Shaykh Muḥammad al-Khuḍari in Egypt has permitted. I am the first to object to it, and I see that the complete abolition [of the Caliphate] is preferable. . . . But the mass of the Muslims [he goes on], insist on a Caliph, and for that reason there has to be an election. You are asking for all the canonical conditions but it is impossible to realise them. I will go

> further. I will say that there is not a single man in Islam who fulfils all the conditions if we were to observe the Canon Law.

He then supports his point by going over all the existing possible candidates. Abdul Majīd has undoubtedly the largest number of electors but he lacks the political power and force ; Imām Yaḥya would score on most points but the majority of Muslims do not see him as the ruler with the necessary organized state and army, some do not even regard him as a Sunni. Ibn as-Sa'ūd is in the opinion of the Muslims just a small Amīr and a Wahhābi whom the Sunnis will reject ; Ḥusayn has one or two points in his favour but he is even weaker than Ibn as-Sa'ūd, he is notorious for his British sympathies, and he is hated by the majority of the Muslims. The Afghani Amīr would be largely acceptable but he is so far away and his is not a great state. There remains only the ruler of Egypt, says Shakīb, and the principal objection is that Egypt is not fully independent and that the Indians and a section of the Egyptian will not elect him. Then there is the possibility of electing an 'Alim with the necessary qualities which is also quite canonical. Such 'Ulamā do exist—he mentions for instance Shaykh ash-Sharīf as-Sanūsi (d. 1933) to whom Muṣṭafa Kamāl offered the spiritual Caliphate.[32] But this he says is impossible because it is impossible for an 'Alim to command group feeling, 'Aṣabiyya, and authority. On the question of 'Aṣabiyya Shakīb Arslān disagrees with Rashīd Riḍā who criticized Ibn Khaldūn for making group feeling the basis for every monarchy and every social act. Shakīb argues that if this group feeling had not been important then how would Qurayshi descent as a condition be explained. He writes very forcefully that any suggestion to be made at the congress which was being planned, no matter how well-supported by canonical requirements, would remain purely ink on paper unless supported by the existence of a powerful Amirate with an army and all the paraphernalia of power. After describing all the difficulties involved, Shakīb Arslān points out that

> the throne which is most worthy of the Caliphate is unquestionably the Egyptian although its holder is not a Qurayshi. . . . It is not advisable [he writes], to be too strict about these conditions, because in reality there is no Caliphate except of the Rashidūn and of 'Umar ibn Abdul Azīz ; after that the Caliphs never fulfilled all the required conditions. If this was the case in the glory of Islam what else can you expect today?

He also makes the point that a congress is a good idea because the pilgrimage in reality is not designed for the Muslims of different parts to meet each other and to discuss questions of importance to Islam, but is merely an opportunity for the Meccans to exploit the pilgrims. It is fitting, he adds, that the congress should take place in Cairo because Egypt in spite of all that is being said is an Arab land *par excellence* ; to have a series of conference, he adds, would be a scandal, and if after all this publicity the projected congress at Cairo is cancelled then the whole thing would prove a mockery.[33]

Rashīd Riḍā could well see for himself all the practical difficulties so well presented to him by Shakīb Arslān. His ambivalence in discussing the Caliphate resulted from the fact that he had to adapt the requirements of the Canon Law to the actual situation and to his own Salafi beliefs. All that he could give in the last resort as attributes to his Caliph was in fact a religious and a judicial function. The utopian hope of restoring through the Caliphate a real Islamic Government based on consultation, Shūra, to which all the Muslim states would pay allegiance did not prevent him from concerning himself with the practical side. The very important and immediate function in his opinion was the duty of the Imām as well as of every Muslim to work towards a renaissance of Muslim culture which, in fact, meant the necessity to encourage the study of classical Arabic literature and the arabization of the school curricula. The Imām more than any other Muslim must be the tool for a religious reformation, i.e. to purify religion of the popular superstitions, innovations, the cult of the saints which had deformed it, to revive the Sunna, and to develop as much as possible through a return to the origins of Islam, the sense of Islamic solidarity and fraternity. To go back to the sources of Islam, the Qur'ān and the Sunna, to reopen the doors of Ijtihād, to readapt the Sharī'ah to the needs of modern life without altering it is the essence of Rashīd Riḍā's modernism. The unification of the four rites would follow naturally from this Ijtihād. He saw within Islam the conservative faction who could not understand that Islam had reached that point of decadence that it must renew itself in order to survive, and the secularists who would do away with Islamic institutions.

An alternative doctrine is that of Shaykh 'Alī 'Abd ur-Rāziq, a Qāḍi of the Egyptian courts in whose book *al-Islām wa Uṣūl al-Ḥukm* (1925) we can find the best example of the inroads into traditional theology made by the political secularism of Turkey, the historical criticism and political thought of the West. The political situation of Egypt may have played a part in his argument but it would not necessarily have made him take this line if he had not really looked upon the Caliphate in this way. 'Alī 'Abd ur-Rāziq gives a novel interpretation of Prophecy by saying that it was confined to theology, ethics and ritual and that Muḥammad never intended to found a particular form of government for a specific political organization. Islam, he maintains, is purely spiritual and ethical and does not discuss the Caliphate any more than it has discussed socialism and bolshevism. He admits that Muḥammad did create the rudiments of a state when he organized his small community in Medina, but he maintains that this was a human but passing act which was not part of his mission. It is simple to proceed from these premises and to prove that the Caliphate is not part of Islam and that its institution is therefore not a religious duty. He is thus led to revise the premises of moderate orthodoxy concerning the Caliphate and to insist that every state rests on force and on the desire to dominate ; on the other hand the Muslim rulers requiring a cloak of legitimacy had obtained from the eager docility of the Fuqahā' the legalisation of their rule by means of the juridical apparatus of the Caliphate. This book created such a storm in Egypt that a decision was unanimously taken by a committee of twenty-four 'Ulamā under the chairmanship of Shaykh al-Azhar to expel 'Alī 'Abd ur-Rāziq from the body of the 'Ulamā. Although it has been amply proved that political pressures were the decisive factors in this decision,[34] it is nonetheless interesting to list here the steps in his argument that the committee objected to :

1. He made the Islamic Sharī'ah purely spiritual without any connexion to the government or the executive power in temporal affairs.

2. He says that the Prophet's wars, Jihād, were for the sake of mere dominion and not for the sake of religion nor in order to spread his religious message to the world.

3. He says that government at the time of the Prophet was subject to obscurity, mystery, confusion or incompleteness and giving rise to perplexity.

4. He says that the Prophet's mission was merely to announce the Sharīʻah without reference to government and the executive power.

5. He denies that there was consensus on the part of the Companions of the Prophet on the necessity for the Muslims for someone who will bear responsibility for their affairs both religious and temporal.

6. He denies that the Judical function is a canonical duty.

7. He says that the government of Abu Bakr and the Rāshidī after him was not a religious government.[35]

The decline of Muslim rule in India especially after British occupation and the final victory of England over the Muslim Raj in the middle of the nineteenth century placed the Indian Muslims in a position of inferiority which made them search for a symbol of strength and power. This, together with the growth of communication, brought them into greater contact with the Ottoman Caliph who was then conducting a clever form of propaganda which Britain came to encourage. Because of her enmity to Russia at the time, Britain took up a pro-Ottoman line and promoted among the Indian Muslims loyalty to the Ottoman Caliph who, in his turn, took advantage of the position by spreading his propaganda and by exploiting the false notion of the Caliphate put out by Europeans. The Indian Muslims slowly came to look upon the Ottoman Caliph as the supreme head of Islam ; at the beginning of the War of 1914 there was a widespread belief in India that the Sultan-Caliph of Turkey was the Caliph of the Muslims. The friendship between Britain and Turkey did not last very long. This created an awkward situation during the War, but in spite of the declaration of Jihād on the part of the Caliph, the British Government was able to prevent any significant amount of Muslim disaffection in India and Indian Muslims fought under British command. The shock to the Indians however came at the end of the War when they finally discovered that what they were fighting for resulted in the dismemberment of the Ottoman Empire and the decline of the Caliphate which had become for them the symbol of Muslim strength and dominion, all the more precious that they themselves had lost it nearly a century earlier.

At the same time local Indian politics at the end of the War were in a disturbed condition and anti-British Muslim leaders like the brothers Muḥammad (1878–1931) and Shaukat (1873–1938?) ‘Alī who had just been released from prison and Abu‘l-Kalām Azād (1888–1958) took up the question of the Caliphate and the fate of the Ottoman Empire as an additional grievance against the British Government.[36] They argued that to destroy the Ottoman Caliphate was to touch the Muslims in their most intimate religious beliefs. A series of All-India Khilāfat conferences took place in 1919 and a delegation was taken by the 'Alī Brothers to London to plead that the dismemberment of the Empire as planned for the Sèvres Treaty was contrary to the Law of Islam. But this proved ineffective and the 'Alī Brothers on their return to India preached that the Government of India had trampled the Law of Islam and that India was now the land of War and that the duty of Muslims was to leave India for a country where Islam was supreme. Multitudes of Muslims left their homes and flocked to Aghanistan but many were disappointed because they were turned back at the borders ; this movement left thousands of people homeless and penniless and is one sad instance of the charged feelings prevalent among the Muslims in India around 1920. The Sèvres Treaty was considered a clear breach of Allied promises and Gandhi who had his own campaign to conduct against the British encouraged the 'Alī Brothers to join forces with him, which they did. They of course had no real sympathy for his non-violence campaign but they were prepared to use his help in order to further their case against Britain. But this alliance did not last very long and the usual slaughter and bloodshed between Hindu and Muslim soon broke out in 1921 at Moplah in Malabar.

In Turkey however other policies were being

followed of which the Indian Muslims, immersed as they were in their own troubles, seemed to be absolutely ignorant. Great rejoicing followed the news of Muṣṭafà Kamāl's victories over the Greeks, and he came to be looked upon as the saviour of the Caliphate and of Islam. When he abolished the Sultanate in 1922, the All-India Khilāfatists and the Jam'iyat al-'Ulamā passed a resolution declaring their confidence in Muṣṭafà Kamāl and approving the action of the GNA in treating Wahīd ud-Dīn as having forfeited office and in electing Abdul Majīd in his place. The withholding of temporal power was passed over in silence. The law of October 1923 however which shook the position of the Caliphate still further occasioned an unfortunate situation which precipitated the downfall of Abdul Majīd. The Agha Khan, Sir Sultan Muḥammad Shah (1877–1956) and Amīr 'Alī (1849–1928) who had championed the cause of Turkey faithfully with Great Britain felt it their duty to write to the Turkish Prime Minister to draw attention to the 'disturbing effects that the uncertain position of the Caliph Imam was having among the Sunni community' and to urge for the 'imminent necessity for maintaining the religious and moral solidarity of Islam by placing the Caliph-Imamate on a basis which would command the confidence and esteem of the Muslim nations'. Through a series of misunderstandings this letter appeared in the Turkish press before it reached Muṣṭafà Kamāl and aroused his anger.[37] In January 1924 the Jam'iyat al-'Ulamā expressed the hope that the status of the Caliph should be referred to a congress. The abolition of the Caliphate in 1924 finally undermined the Khilāfat movement. The Indians' only hope then was that the Congress of the Caliphate to be held in Cairo would solve the problem.

On March 25, 1924, the chief 'Ulamā of Egypt made a statement to the effect that the ' Caliphate of Abdul Majīd was not a legal Caliphate, since the Islamic religion does not recognize a Caliphate in the terms laid down for him by the Turkish Government and which he accepted. Hence the allegiance Bay'āh paid to him by Muslims was not valid in Islamic Law.'[38] They then put forth the idea of an Islamic congress for the Caliphate to meet in Cairo in 1925 to which representatives from all the Islamic peoples should be invited. In fact the meeting had to be postponed till May 1926, and when it did take place it was not representative of all the Islamic peoples—some of the delegates attended only in their private capacity—nor did it give a final answer to this question.[39]

There is enough evidence now to prove that the Congress was planned and encouraged through the instigation of King Fuād who was secretly hoping to gain the Caliphate for himself, although when it came to open and direct enquiry he had, because of the state of Egyptian parties and politics, to deny any personal interest in the matter. It was the original hope of the organizers of the Congress to proclaim King Fuād Caliph but this was not feasible because of the opposition both inside and outside Egypt. The Wafd under Zaghlūl did not wish the King to gain more power and the Liberal Constitutionalists were then opposed in principle to a situation which would introduce religion into politics. The case of ʻAlī ʻAbd ur-Rāziq was deeply involved in all this; his connexions were all with the liberal Constitutionalists and the timing of the book was most inconvenient for the King and his ambitions, which may lead one to believe that publication was made at that time partly with an eye on the political situation. Outside Egypt Husayn had had his disappointed hopes and was not likely to support Fuād's claims, Ibn as-Saʻūd was also opposed partly perhaps because he entertained hopes for himself and partly because he did not want to enhance the prestige of a rival. As for the Indian Muslims, they were so shocked and bewildered by the Turkish action that they were bound to bring up Abdul Majīd's claims into any serious discussion dealing with the problem, and in fact when the Jerusalem Congress of 1931 was being organized by the Muftī of Jerusalem, Shaukat ʻAlī made a statement to the effect that there would be no reason to discuss the question of the Caliphate because there was still a living Caliph, namely Abdul Majīd. The Cairo meeting was postponed in order to smooth out difficulties but nothing was achieved through this delay and when the conference finally took place in May 1926, it was clear that there was no question of electing a Caliph.

Arrangements had gone so far that the organizers perhaps felt like Shakīb Arslān that to cancel the Congress after all the publicity that had taken place would be disastrous for Egypt and the Islamic world. The delegates came in their private capacity and Shaykh Muṣṭafà al-Marāghi, one of the organizers and Fuād's supporter, had to explain that 'circumstances had changed since the Congress was first mooted and the proclamation of a Caliph by the Congress was out of the question'. It seems that when the organizers found out that it was impossible to proclaim Fuād Caliph and each delegation inclined to having the ruler of their own country proclaimed, it was decided that the best way to preserve Islamic unity and Egyptian dignity was to wind up the Congress and forestall any damaging resolutions; the pretext for this was that not all Muslim nations were represented. The Congress which only met four times then affirmed that a Caliphate was obligatory but that it was impossible to establish one immediately and therefore decided to found branches of the Congress to meet in different countries in order to prepare other congresses to settle the question. In spite of the failure of this Congress the question lingered on in the minds of some leaders. The Muftī of Jerusalem, Hāj Amīn al-Ḥusayni, no doubt in order to strengthen himself *vis-à-vis* his Arab rivals and the Zionists, called for a Congress to be held in Jerusalem at the end of 1931. This greatly disturbed Fuād who was worried by the rumour that the Caliphate question would be discussed and probably a Caliph proclaimed. The agitation which followed was so strong that the Muftī had to visit Cairo personally and give both verbal and written assurances that the question would not be discussed. From then till Fuād's death in 1936 there was silence about this problem but the accession of Fāruq to the Egyptian throne brought up the question again. Fāruq tried to exploit the sympathy shown to him by adopting at his coronation some of the Ottoman ceremonial used at the accession of a new Caliph; he was strongly opposed in this by his Wafdist Prime Minister Muṣṭafà al-Naḥḥās Pāsha. The joint efforts of Shaykh al-Marāghi and of Fāruq to proclaim the latter Caliph came up against strong internal and external opposition; but hope lingered on until Fāruq's downfall, for how otherwise is one to explain that as late as May 1952 Qurayshi descent through the female line was made up for him?[40] Since then the proclamations of republics in so many Muslim countries seem to indicate a more secular trend rather than a revival of the Caliphate.

REFERENCES TO AUTHORITIES

CHAPTER I

1 (p. 9) Henry Osborn Taylor, The Mediaeval Mind, vol. ii, p. 303. (London, 1914.)

2 (p. 12) I. Goldziher, Muhammedanische Studien, vol. ii, p. 19 sqq.

3 (p. 12) Traditionis nomen accommodatum est a Theologis ad significandam tantum doctrinam non scriptam. Cardinal R. Bellarmin, Disputationes de controversiis christianae fidei, t. i, p. 147. (Romae, 1832.)

4 (p. 15) Bukhārī, ed. Krehl, vol. i, p. 181, ll. 4–5 ; Kanz ul-'Ummāl, vol. iv, nr. 2700.

5 (p. 16) Goldziher, op. cit., vol. ii, pp. 277–8.

CHAPTER II

1 (p. 19) Memoirs of Edmund Ludlow, ed. C. H. Firth, vol. ii, p. 44. (Oxford, 1894.)

2 (p. 19) Lammens, Le 'triumvirat' Abou Bakr, 'Omar et Abou 'Obaida. Mélanges de la Faculté Orientale, Beyrouth, t. iv, pp. 113 sqq.

3 (p. 21) The circumstances connected with these two appointments have been fully investigated by Caetani, Annali dell' Islām, 11 A.H., § 55 sqq., and 13 A.H., §§ 75 sqq., 133 sqq.

4 (p. 21) Annali dell' Islām, vol. v, p. 48.

5 (p. 24) Caetani, Studi di Storia Orientale, t. i, pp. 281–2.

6 (p. 27) Kanz, vol. iii, nr. 2570.

7 (p. 32) Mas'ūdī, Kitāb at-Tanbīh, p. 236, ll. 15–16.

8 (p. 32) Ibn Khaldūn, Prolégomènes, trad. De Slane, i, p. 462.

9 (p. 35) Caetani, Annali dell' Islām, 11 A.H., § 16.

10 (p. 39) Mufaḍḍal ibn Abi 'l-Faḍā'il, Histoire des Sultans Mamlouks, ed. E. Blochet, p. [506].

11 (p. 41) Ibn Khaldūn, op. cit., i, p. 463.

CHAPTER III

1 (p. 47) Kanz, vol. vi, nr. 3452.

2 (p. 47) id. vi, nr. 3469.

3 (p. 47) id. vi, nr. 3429.

4 (p. 47) id. iii, nr. 2983.

5 (p. 48) id. iii, nr. 2999.

6 (p. 48) id. iii, nr. 2580.

7 (p. 49) id. iii, nr. 3008.

8 (p. 49) id. iii, nr. 3005.

9 (p. 49) id. iii, nr. 3003.

10 (p. 50) id. iii, nr. 2786.

11 (p. 51) Goldziher, Du sens propre des expressions Ombre de Dieu, Khalife de Dieu, pour désigner les chefs dans l'Islam. Revue de l'Histoire des Religions, tome xxxv (1897).

12 (p. 51) Ṭabarī, iii, p. 1387, ll. 13–14.

13 (p. 51) Kanz, iii, nr. 2237.

14 (p. 51) ed. H. Hirschfeld, xx, l. 9. The application of the phrase to the Prophet himself would appear to be of a much later date, e.g. Ibn Ẓafar, Sulwān al-muṭā', p. 24, l. 3 a.f. (Tunis, 1279 A.H.)

15 (p. 51) Goldziher, op. cit., p. 6.

16 (p. 51) Māwardī, ed. Enger, p. 22 fin.

17 (p. 51) Ṭabari, iii, p. 426, l. 16.

18 (p. 52) Suyūṭī, Ta'rīkh ul-Khulafā (ed. Cairo, 1305 A.H.), pp. 6–7.

19 (p. 53) id., p. 3.

20 (p. 53) id., p. 7.

21 (p. 53) Of Manṣūr (754–775) it was said : 'The majesty of the Khilāfat did not prevent him from humbling himself before the law.' Fragmenta historicorum arabicorum, ed. De Goeje, p. 269, ll. 5–6.

CHAPTER IV

1 (p. 62) Ibn ul-Athīr, viii, p. 222. (ed. Cairo, 1290 A.H.)

2 (p. 67) Quṭb ud-Dīn. Chroniken der Stadt Mekka, ed. F. Wüstenfeld, vol. iii, pp. 168–9.

3 (p. 69) C. Snouck Hurgronje, Mekka, vol. i, p. 59.

CHAPTER V

1 (p. 71) Māwardī, al-Aḥkām us-sulṭāniyyah (ed. Enger), pp. 5–7.

2 (p. 72) id., p. 23.

3 (p. 73) Chronologie orientalischer Völker, p. 132.

4 (p. 74) Chahár Maqála, ed. Mirza Muḥammad, p. 10; Revised Translation by Edward G. Browne, p. 11. (Gibb Memorial Series.)

5 (p. 76) Ibn Khaldūn, Prolégomènes, i, pp. 386–8, 394–9, 423–4.

CHAPTER VI

1 (p. 78) Bryce, Holy Roman Empire (ed. 1918), pp. 229, 272–3.

2 (p. 79) H. M. Elliot, History of India, vol. ii, p. 24.

3 (p. 80) v. Appendix D.

4 (p. 80) Barthold, Міръ Ислама, i, p. 221.

5 (p. 80) Houtsma, Recueil de textes relatifs à l'histoire des Seljoucides, ii, pp. 241–2.

6 (p. 81) Fragmenta historicorum arabicorum, p. 101, l. 11.

7 (p. 82) C. d'Ohsson, Histoire des Mongols, t. iii, pp. 251–4.

8 (p. 82) Suyūṭī, Ḥusn ul-Muḥāḍarah, vol. ii, pp. 53 sqq., 57.

9 (p. 86) Al-Khazrajī, The Pearl-strings, Text i, p. 55; Translation i, pp. 98–9. (Gibb Memorial Series iii.)

10 (p. 87) Ṭabaqāt-i-Nāṣirī, trans. Raverty, p. 1259. In a similar manner the Samānids had continued to recite the Khuṭbah in the name of Ṭā'i' for eight years after his deposition. (Abū Shujā', ed. Amedroz and Margoliouth, p. 332.)

11 (p. 87) H. N. Wright, Catalogue of the Coins in the Indian Museum, Calcutta, vol. ii, p. 36.

12 (p. 88) id., p. 38.

CHAPTER VII

1 (p. 94) Suyūṭī, Ḥusn ul-Maḥāḍarah, vol. ii, p. 59 sqq.

2 (p. 98) id., pp. 62–3.

3 (p. 98) Max van Berchem, Inschriften aus Syrien, Mesopotamien und Kleinasien, p. 5.

CHAPTER VIII

1 (p. 99) Khalīl ibn Shāhīn aẓ-Ẓāhirī, Zubdat kashf al-mamālik, ed. P. Ravaisse, p. 89.

2 (p. 100) Suyūṭī, Ta'rīkh ul-Khulafā, p. 197.

3 (p. 100) Weil, Geschichte des Abbasidenchalifats in Egypten, i, p. 406, n. 2.

4 (p. 100) Al-Fāsī, sub anno 815. Chroniken der Stadt Mekka, vol. ii, pp. 294–5.

5 (p. 101) Weil, op. cit., ii, pp. 126–8.

6 (p. 101) Suyūṭī, Ta'rīkh ul-Khulafā, p. 164.

7 (p. 102) Khalīl ibn Shāhīn, op. cit., p. 89.

8 (p. 102) Suyūṭī, op. cit., p. 164.

9 (p. 102) Maqrīzī, Histoire d'Égypte, ed. E. Blochet, p. 76.

10 (p. 103) Barthold, op. cit., i, p. 359.

11 (p. 104) Ẓiyā ud-Dīn Baranī, Ta'rīkh-i-Fīrūz Shāhī, p. 491 sqq.; Ibn Baṭṭūṭa, i, p. 364.

12 (p. 105) H. N. Wright, op. cit., vol. ii, p. 52 fin.

13 (p. 105) Futūḥāt-i-Fīrūz Shāhī. H. M. Elliot, History of India, vol. iii, p. 387.

14 (p. 106) 'Abd ur-Razzāq as-Samarqandī, Maṭla' us-sa'dayn wa majma' ul-baḥrayn, fol. 9 b. (British Museum MS. Or. 1291.)

15 (p. 106) J. von Hammer, Geschichte des Osmanischen Reiches², vol. i, p. 195; M. d'Ohsson, Tableau de l'Empire Othoman, i, pp. 233–4.

16 (p. 106) Barthold, op. cit., i, p. 360.

17 (p. 106) Aḥmad Firīdūn Bey, Munsha'āt us-Salāṭīn. (Constantinople, 1264–5 A.H.) vol. i, p. 130, l. 25.

CHAPTER IX

1 (p. 107) Kanz ul-'Ummāl, vol. iii, nr. 3152.

2 (p. 108) Prolégomènes, i, p. 424 init.

3 (p. 108) Chroniken der Stadt Mekka, vol. iii, p. 182, l. 11.

4 (p. 108) id. iii, p. 184, ll. 5–6.

5 (p. 108) Ibn Khaldūn, Prolégomènes, i, p. 396.

6 (p. 109) L. Cahun, Introduction à l'histoire de l'Asie, p. 244 &c.

7 (p. 111) Rashīd ud-Dīn, Jāmi' ut-tawārīkh, fol. 327 b. (India Office Library MS. Ethé 17.)

8 (p. 111) Mufaḍḍal ibn Abi 'l-Faḍā'il, Histoire des Sultans Mamlouks, ed. E. Blochet, p. [483].

9 (p. 111) 'Abd ur-Razzāq, Maṭla' us-Sa'dayn, fol. 19 b. (British Museum MS. Or. 1291.)

10 (p. 112) Firīdūn, op. cit., i, p. 144, l. 7 a.f.

11 (p. 112) id. i, p. 184, l. 11.

12 (p. 112) id. i, p. 143, l. 4 a.f.

13 (p. 113) Weil, Geschichte des Abbasidenchalifats in Egypten, ii, pp. 201–2.

14 (p. 113) Partially translated by Quatremère, in Notices et Extraits, xiv, 1.

15 (p. 113) E. Thomas, Chronicles of the Pathan Kings of Delhi, pp. 326–9.

16 (p. 114) Barthold, op. cit., i, pp. 362–3.

17 (p. 114) Hāfiẓ Abrū, Ta'rīkh-i-Shāh Rukh, fol. 2 b. (India Office Library MS. Ethé 171.)

18 (p. 114) Zubdat ut-tawārīkh, fol. 5 b. (British Museum Or. 2774.)

19 (p. 114) Ta'rīkh-i-Shāh Rukh, fol. 3 b. (I.O. Ethé 171.)

20 (p. 116) Ibn Baṭṭūṭa, i, p. 4 ; ii, p. 382.

21 (p. 116) C. Huart, Épigraphie arabe d'Asie Mineure. Revue Sémitique, t. iii, p. 369.

22 (p. 116) Khazā'in ul-Futūḥ, fol. 2. (British Museum MS. Add. 16838.)

23 (p. 117) H. N. Wright, op. cit., vol. ii, pp. 43–4.

24 (p. 117) Tadhkiratu 'sh-Shu'arā, ed. Edward G. Browne, p. 306, l. 5.

25 (p. 117) Ẓafar-nāmah, fol. 5, l. 3. (British Museum MS. Add. 23980.)

26 (p. 117) Franz Babinger, Schejch Bedr ed-Din. Der Islam, vol. xi, p. 41.

27 (p. 117) Firīdūn, op. cit., i, p. 271, l. 11 a.f.

28 (p. 118) Akhlāq-i-Jalālī (ed. Lucknow, 1868), p. 9, ll. 4–5.

29 (p. 118) Firīdūn, op. cit., i, p. 341, l. 10.

30 (p. 118) Barthold, op. cit., i, p. 363.

31 (p. 118) Firīdūn, op. cit., i, p. 277, l. 1.

32 (p. 118) Tadhkiratu 'sh-Shu'arā, p. 458, ll. 11–12.

33 (p. 118) Max van Berchem, Corpus Inscriptionum Arabicarum, i, pp. 46, 91, &c.

34 (p. 119) Barthold, Записки Вост. Отд. Арх. Общ., t. xv, p. 223.

35 (p. 119) Supplément turc 635.

36 (p. 120) Harl. 3273, Or. 1376, and Add. 7918.

37 (p. 120) Prolégomènes, i, p. 387.

CHAPTER X

1 (p. 122) Alfārābīs Abhandlung über den Musterstaat, ed. Fr. Dieterici. Leiden, 1895.

2 (p. 123) Thier und Mensch, ed. Dieterici, p. 27, ll. 14–19.

3 (p. 124) A. von Kremer, Geschichte der herrschenden Ideen des Islam, pp. 92–4.

4 (p. 125) Siyāsat-nāmah, ed. Schefer, p. 5, ll. 7–8 a.f.

5 (p. 128) Zubdat ut-tawārīkh, fol. 5 b. (British Museum MS. Or. 2774.)

CHAPTER XI

1 (p. 129) Firīdūn, op. cit., i, pp. 120, l. 12 a.f.; 170, l. 4 a.f. &c.

2 (p. 130) id. i, p. 93, ll. 22, 23.

3 (p. 130) id. i, p. 94, ll. 10–16.

4 (p. 131) id. i, p. 95 fin.–96, l. 1.

5 (p. 131) id. i, p. 97, l. 1.

6 (p. 131) id. i, p. 100, ll. 10, 8 a.f.

7 (p. 132) id. i, p. 118, ll. 3–2 a.f.

8 (p. 132) id. i, p. 120, ll. 13–12 a.f.

9 (p. 133) J. von Hammer, Geschichte des Osmanischen Reiches², vol. i, p. 280.

10 (p. 133) Firīdūn, op. cit., i, pp. 139–43.

11 (p. 133) id. i, p. 144, l. 15.

12 (p. 133) id. i, p. 151, l. 12.

13 (p. 133) id. i, p. 145, l. 13 a.f.

14 (p. 133) id. i, p. 148, ll. 9–10, fihrist-i-kitāb-i-sultanat wa dībācha-i-risāla-i-khilāfat.

15 (p. 134) id. i, p. 159 fin.–160.

16 (p. 134) id. i, p. 160, l. 3 a.f.

17 (p. 134) id. i, p. 170, ll. 5–4 a.f.
18 (p. 135) id. i, p. 183, l. 14.
19 (p. 135) id. i, p. 209, ll. 11–12.
20 (p. 135) id. i, p. 267, l. 12.
21 (p. 136) id. i, p. 268, l. 11.
22 (p. 136) id. i, p. 272, ll. 17–18.
23 (p. 136) id. i, p. 276, l. 5.
24 (p. 136) id. i, p. 308, ll. 14–16.
25 (p. 136) id. i, p. 322, ll. 3–1 a.f.
26 (p. 137) id. i, p. 340, ll. 12–11 a.f.
27 (p. 137) id. i, p. 341, ll. 8, 5 a.f.
28 (p. 137) id. i, p. 343, ll. 21–28.
29 (p. 138) id. i, p. 345, ll. 9, 11.
30 (p. 138) id. i, p. 354, l. 21.
31 (p. 138) id. i, p. 349, l. 22.
32 (p. 138) id. i, p. 365, l. 4.
33 (p. 138) id. i, p. 368, l. 2.
34 (p. 138) id. i, p. 368, l. 16 a.f.
35 (p. 138) id. i, p. 358, l. 11.

CHAPTER XII

1 (p. 140) Ibn Iyās, Ta'rīkh Miṣr, vol. iii, p. 49, wa ajlasahu wa jalasa bayna yadayhi.

2 (p. 141) id. iii, p. 98 fin.

3 (p. 141) id. iii, p. 105.

4 (p. 142) id. iii, p. 229.

5 (p. 142) Chroniken der Stadt Mekka, vol. iii, p. 185, l. 3.

6 (p. 142) Weil, Geschichte des Abbasidenchalifats in Egypten, vol. ii, p. 435.

7 (p. 143) Firīdūn, op. cit., i, pp. 398–406 and 406–48. In the longer of these two reports, the 'Abbasid Caliph of Egypt' is merely mentioned in connexion with the embassy to Tūmān Bay in March 1517. (id. p. 435, ll. 19–20.)

8 (p. 143) Barthold, Міръ Ислама, i, pp. 372, 381.

9 (p. 144) Ta'rīkh Miṣr, iii, p. 176, l. 12.

10 (p. 144) Firīdūn, op. cit., i, pp. 376–9, dated Muḥarram 923 (Jan.–Feb. 1517).

11 (p. 144) id. i, p. 379 init.

12 (p. 145) Quṭb ud-Dīn. Chroniken der Stadt Mekka, iii, pp. 278–9.

13 (p. 145) J. von Hammer, Geschichte², vol. i, p. 702, n. 5.

14 (p. 146) Firīdūn, op. cit., i, p. 383, l. 8.

15 (p. 147) e.g. A. von Kremer, Geschichte der herrschenden Ideen des Islams, p. 423 ; G. Weil, Geschichte des Abbasidenchalifats in Egypten, ii, p. 435 ; A. Müller, Der Islam im Morgen- und Abendland, i, p. 641.

16 (p. 148) Weil, op. cit., ii, p. 395.

17 (p. 151) id. i, p. 314.

18 (p. 151) Firīdūn, op. cit., i, p. 128, ll. 20–24.

19 (p. 151) Yūsuf ibn Taghrībirdī, Ḥawādith ud-Duhūr, fol. 13 b. (British Museum MS. Add. 23294.)

20 (p. 152) Al-Fāsī. Chroniken der Stadt Mekka, ii, p. 295, ll. 6–3 a.f.

21 (p. 152) Quṭb ud-Dīn. Chroniken, iii, p. 247 fin.

22 (p. 153) C. Snouck Hurgronje, Mekka, vol. i, p. 102.

23 (p. 153) Quṭb ud-Dīn, op. cit., iii, p. 286, l. 2 a.f.

24 (p. 154) Firīdūn, i, p. 406, ll. 15–17.

25 (p. 154) id. i, p. 380, ll. 15–16.

26 (p. 154) id. i, p. 381, l. 4 a.f.

27 (p. 154) id. i, p. 382, l. 19.

28 (p. 155) id. i, p. 383, l. 5 a.f.

29 (p. 155) id. i, p. 351 fin.

30 (p. 155) id. i, p. 348 fin.–349, l. 1.

31 (p. 155) id. i, pp. 363, 379.

32 (p. 155) id. i, pp. 392, 394.

33 (p. 155) id. i, p. 395.

34 (p. 155) id. i, p. 448, ll. 16–17.

35 (p. 156) id. i, p. 448, l. 14.

36 (p. 156) Max van Berchem, Corpus Inscriptionum Arabicarum, i, p. 606.

37 (p. 157) Barthold, op. cit., i, p. 392.

38 (p. 157) Chroniken, iii, p. 249.

39 (p. 158) Firīdūn, i, p. 449, l. 19.

40 (p. 158) id., ll. 14–15.

41 (p. 158) Chroniken der Stadt Mekka, iii, p. 329, l. 9.

42 (p. 158) id., p. 367, l. 9.

43 (p. 158) id., p. 390, l. 9.

CHAPTER XIII

1 (p. 159) S. Lane-Poole, Catalogue of Indian Coins in the British Museum. The Mogul Emperors, p. lxxiii.

2 (p. 160) Munsha'āt wa ba'ḍ waqā'i'-i-Sulṭān Sulaymān Khān, foll. 257–8. (National-Bibliothek, Vienna. MS. H. O. 50.)

3 (p. 161) 'Abdī Ṣārī Efendi, Dastūr ul-Inshā, fol. 28. (National-Bibliothek, Vienna. MS. H. O. 167.)

4 (p. 162) id., foll. 128–9;

5 (p. 162) Shāh 'Ālam Nāmah, p. 16, ll. 5–6. (Calcutta, 1912.)

CHAPTER XIV

1 (p. 163) 'Aqā'id, ed. Cureton, p. 4, l. 4 a.f.

2 (p. 163) M. d'Ohsson, Tableau général de l'Empire Othoman (8vo ed.), t. i, p. 212.

3 (p. 164) ed. Constantinople, 1264–5 A.H., vol. i, pp. 2–4.

4 (p. 165) C. A. Nallino, Appunti sulla natura del 'Califfato' in genere e sul presunto 'Califfato Ottomano', p. 16.

5 (p. 166) Barthold, op. cit., i, p. 395.

6 (p. 167) Historia Hierosolymitana. Gesta Dei per Francos, t. i, p. 57. (Hanoviae, 1611.)

7 (p. 168) Sextus filius est nomine Machomet, qui tenet regnum de Baudas, ubi est Papa Saracenorum, qui vocatur Kabatus, sive Caliphas ; qui colitur, adoratur, et tenetur in lege eorum tanquam Romanus Episcopus apud nos, qui non potest videri nisi bis in mense, quando hic cum suis vadit ad Machomet Deum Saracenorum. Et inclinato capite et facta oratione in lege eorum antequam exeant de templo, splendide comedunt et bibunt, et sic revertitur Caliphas coronatus ad palatium suum. Iste Deus Machomet visitatur quotidie et adoratur, sicut visitatur et adoratur dominus Papa. In ista civitate de Baudas iste Machomet est Deus, et Calyphas est Papa, quae civitas est caput totius gentis et legis Saracenorum, ut Roma est in populo Christiano. (Jacobi de Vitriaco Historia Hierosolimitana. Gesta Dei per Francos, t. i, p. 1125.)

8 (p. 168) Chronica Maiora, vol. ii, p. 400.

9 (p. 168) The Book of Ser Marco Polo, translated by Sir Henry Yule, 3rd ed., vol. i, p. 63.

10 (p. 169) Petrus Martyr Anglerius, De rebus oceanicis et novo orbe decades, p. 412. (Coloniae, 1574.)

11 (p. 169) Geographisches Wörterbuch, ed. Wüstenfeld, vol. ii, p. 867, ll. 7–9.

12 (p. 169) Mir'āt uz-zamān. Recueil des Historiens des Croisades, t. iii, p. 560.

13 (p. 170) Prolégomènes, i, pp. 474, 476.

14 (p. 170) R. Hartmann, Arabien im Weltkrieg. Petermanns Mitteilungen, 63, p. 55.

15 (p. 170) Ṣubḥ ul-A'shà, vol. v, p. 408 fin.

16 (p. 170) t. i (8vo ed.), pp. 252, 263.

17 (p. 170) id., pp. 215, 237.

18 (p. 171) C. Mirbt, Quellen zur Geschichte des Papsttums^3, pp. 127, 156–7, 365–7, 424.

19 (p. 175) A. de la Jonquière, Histoire de l'empire ottoman^2, ii, pp. 70, 179.

20 (p. 175) Sir Edwin Pears, Life of Abdul Hamid, p. 149.

21 (p. 176) C. Snouck Hurgronje, Verspreide Geschriften, vol. iii, p. 193.

22 (p. 176) A. de la Jonquière, op. cit., ii, p. 183.

23 (p. 177) Edward G. Browne, The Persian Revolution, p. 84.

24 (p. 177) A. de la Jonquière, op. cit., ii, p. 221.

25 (p. 178) Nallino, op. cit., pp. 20–21.

26 (p. 181) L. W. C. van den Berg, De Mohammedaansche Vorsten in Nederlandsch-Indië. (Bijdragen tot de Taal-, Land- en Volkenkunde van Nederlandsch-Indië, liii (1901), pp. 23, 28.)

27 (p. 182) Encyclopedie van Nederlandsch-Indië, 2nd ed., vol. iv, p. 364.

APPENDIX A

1 (p. 187) Edward G. Browne, The Persian Revolution, pp. 372–3.

APPENDIX B

1 (p. 190) A. Ubicini et Pavet de Courteille, État présent de l'Empire Ottoman, pp. 77–8. (Paris, 1876.)

2 (p. 191) Martin Hartmann, in Die Welt des Islams, i, p. 148. (Berlin, 1913.)

3 (p. 192) C. H. Becker, Islampolitik. Die Welt des Islams, iii, p. 103. (Berlin, 1915.)

4 (p. 193) id., p. 113.

5 (p. 194) C. Snouck Hurgronje, The Holy War ‘ made in Germany ’, pp. 16–18. (New York, 1915.)

6 (p. 195) id., pp. 27–9.

7 (p. 196) C. Snouck Hurgronje, Nederland en de Islam, 2nd ed., pp. 67–8. (Leiden, 1915.)

8 (p. 197) id., p. 70.

9 (p. 198) C. Snouck Hurgronje, Mohammedanism, pp. 128–30. (New York, 1916.)

10 (p. 199) C. A. Nallino, op. cit., pp. 5, 6.

11 (p. 200) id., p. 7.

12 (p. 200) id., p. 10.

APPENDIX C

1 (p. 201) Greek Papyri of the British Museum, vol. iv. The Aphrodito Papyri ed. H. G. Bell, pp. xxv, 35 ; C. H. Becker, Islamstudien, i, p. 257.

2 (p. 201) M. d'Ohsson, op. cit., vol. vii, p. 271.

3 (p. 201) J. von Hammer, op. cit., iii, p. 474.

4 (p. 201) Gul-badan Begam, Humāyūn-nāma, ed. Annette S. Beveridge, p. 136.

5 (p. 201) C. Snouck Hurgronje, The Achehnese, pp. 18, 251–2. (Leiden, 1906.)

APPENDIX D

1 (p. 202) C. H. Becker, Beiträge zur Geschichte Ägyptens unter dem Islam, p. 90, n. 6.

2 (p. 202) Prolégomènes, ii, p. 9.

3 (p. 202) Ṭabarī, iii, p. 1894, l. 11.

4 (p. 202) S. Lane-Poole, Mohammadan Dynasties, p. 286.

5 (p. 203) Khalīl ibn Shāhīn, op. cit., p. 89, l. 6 a.f.

6 (p. 203) Max van Berchem, Inschriften aus Syrien, Mesopotamien und Kleinasien, pp. 4, 5, 83, &c. ; Corpus Inscriptionum Arabicarum, v. Index sub voc.

THE ABOLITION OF THE CALIPHATE

1. p. 180 above.

2. p. 173 above.

3. This Fatwā it seems irritated Muṣṭafà Kamāl because of the ill-effects it had on the regular troops ; see *A Speech Delivered by Ghazi Mustapha Kemal President of the Turkish Republic, October 1927*, Leipzig, 1929, p. 401, hereafter referred to as *Speech*.

4. On this law and the discussions relating to it, see Arnold J. Toynbee, *Survey of International Relations, 1925*, vol. I, *The Islamic World since the Peace Settlement*, London. 1927, pp. 50–1.

5. See *Speech*, p. 380. Also article 'Atatürk' in *Islâm Ansiklopedisi*, English translation published by the *Turkish National Commission for UNESCO*, 1963, p. 127. For the objections raised by the opposition and their sudden collapse at Muṣṭafà Kamāl's threat that some heads might fall, see *Speech*, p. 572 ff.

6. *Speech*, p. 582 ff. On a later occasion, in a letter dated January 1924, Muṣṭafà Kamāl objects to the Caliph because he oversteps his limits and indulges in pomp and glory, *Speech*, pp. 681–2.

7. For a full French translation of this document, see *Revue du Monde Musulman* (*RMM*), vol. 59, 1925, pp. 3–81.

8. This seems erroneous. The title Imām emphasizes the religious character of the Caliphate which is recognized by Sunnis and Shi'ites alike. See Emile Tyan, *Institutions du Droit Public Musulman*, vol. I, *Le Califat*, Paris, 1954, p. 484.

9. pp. 70–1 above.

10. *Speech*, pp. 18–20.

11. Toynbee, op. cit., p. 60 and pp. 572–5 for text of these laws.

12. *Speech*, pp. 583–4.

13. *Oriente Moderno*, vol. III, 1923, pp. 408–13, gives a survey of the Turkish press in connexion with the rumours that the Caliph might resign. A press campaign was conducted and the Conservative press printed a communiqué from the Caliph himself saying that he is not responsible for

originating any of these, affirming that his election by the GNA is quite legal and stressing that he does not mix in politics and that he only has the welfare of the Muslims in mind. He referred to the definition of the religious function of the Caliph, a definition which is essential for the dignity of the Caliph. The popular government had been too busy to deal with that but he expressed the hope that a congress of all the Muslim states rumoured to take place might consider this question.

14. Toynbee, op. cit., p. 56.

15. *Speech*, pp. 378–9 ; Muṣṭafà Kamāl expressed his duties to the people as follows : 'To work within our national boundaries for the real happiness and welfare of the nation and the country by, above all, relying on our own strength in order to retain our existence. But not to lead the people to follow fictitious aims, of whatever nature, which would only bring them misfortune, and expect from the civilized world human treatment, friendship based on mutuality.'

16. *Speech*, p. 682.

17. *Oriente Moderno*, 1924, pp. 141–2, where the late Professor Nallino printed part of a statement which Muṣṭafà Kamāl had given to a French publicist. 'Les Turcs sont la seule nation ', Muṣṭafà Kamāl said, ' qui assure effectivement la subsistence du Calife. Ceux qui préconisent le Calife universel se sont abstenus jusqu'à présent de toute contribution. Alors que prétendent-ils ? Que les Turcs supportent seuls les charges de cette institution, et qu'ils soient aussi seuls à respecter l'autorité souveraine du Calife ? La prétention serait excessive . . .' See also *Speech*, p. 591.

18. *Speech*, p. 685.

19. See S. A. Yalman, *Turkey in my Time*, 1956, p. 136 ff. According to Yalman Muṣṭafà Kamāl ordered the editors of seven Turkish dailies in January 1924 to conduct a press campaign preparing public opinion for the abolition of the Caliphate. The papers were to ' attack the government for not realizing the danger to the unity and stability of the country which the continuation of the khalifate constituted ', and ' to put out that the khalifate was obsolete from the standpoint of a modern Turkey, that the prestige attributed to it was a myth, and that the victory of the Turkish nation

would not be complete without a concerted assault on the theocratic influence which blocked progress'. This press campaign aroused the Caliph's concern early on to judge by an exchange of letters between Ismet Pasha, President of the Council of Ministers, and Muṣṭafà Kamāl in January 1924; see *Speech*, p. 681 ff.

20. This is very well analysed by Nallino in an article 'La Fine del Cosī Detto Califfato Ottomano', in *Oriente Moderno*, 1924, pp. 137–53. But in both this article and his *Notes on the Nature of the 'Caliphate' in General and the Alleged 'Ottoman Caliphate'* first published in 1916 (English translation, Rome, 1919) Professor Nallino, because he sees so clearly the absurdity of the Caliphate as exploited by Abdul Ḥamīd and then as presented by the Ankara Government, tends to underestimate the emotional content it had for the Muslims.

21. *Speech*, p. 588 ff.

22. For the desire or unwillingness of Ḥusayn to accept the Bay'āh, see Toynbee, op. cit., p. 65, and Elie Kedourie, 'Egypt and the Caliphate, 1915–1946', in *Journal of the Royal Asiatic Society*, October 1963, pp. 213–14.

23. p. 108 above. See the excellent book of Emile Tyan, *Institutions du Droit Public Musulman*, vol. I, *Le Califat*, Paris, 1954, pp. 361–70, on the necessity of Qurayshi origin.

24. On al-Kawākibī, see Sylvia G. Haim, *The Ideas of a Precursor, 'Abd al-Raḥmān al-Kawākibī (1849–1902), in Relation to the Trend of Muslim-Arab Political Thought*, Ph.D. thesis, Edinburgh, 1953; also idem, 'Blunt and al-Kawākibī', *Oriente Moderno*, vol. XXXV, no. 3, 1955, pp. 132–43.

25. This line of argument is taken up by A. Sanhoury, *Le Califat; Son Evolution vers une Société des Nations Orientale*, Paris, 1926, where he argues that the solution of the problem would be to have an international religious Caliph elected by a general assembly for the Caliphate which would be made up of representatives from every Muslim state and community who would meet in Mecca; this Caliph would be the symbol of an Oriental League of Nations.

26. S. G. Haim, *Arab Nationalism; An Anthology*, Berkeley, 1962, pp. 28–9, and Kedourie, loc. cit., pp. 228–9.

27. S. G. Haim, thesis, p. 91 ff.

28. See *Oriente Moderno*, vol. IV, 1924, pp. 229–39 for reactions to Ḥusayn's Caliphate.

29. Kedourie, loc. cit., pp. 215–16 ; also for the political desires and alignments.

30. Henri Laoust, *Le Califat dans la Doctrine de Rashīd Riḍā*, Beirut, 1938, p. 2. The book which gives a full French translation of *al-Khilāfa wa'l-Imāma al-'Uẓma* has a most concise and perspicacious preface.

31. Kedourie, loc. cit., p. 242.

32. Kedourie, loc. cit., p. 222.

33. Aḥmad ash-Sharabāṣi, *Amīr al-Bayān Shakīb Arslān*, Cairo, 1963, vol. II, p. 655 ff. ; also p. 666 ff. where he maintains the same views in a letter dated July 8, 1924. He also points out that if Abdul Majīd's Caliphate were to be rejected by the Muslims, the result would be that—as things stand—not one but ten Caliphs would be proclaimed.

34. Kedourie, loc. cit., esp. pp. 223–6.

35. Al-Azhar, *Ḥukm Hay'at Kibār al-'Ulamā fi Kitāb al-Islām wa Uṣūl al-Ḥukm*, Cairo, 1925. For a summary of the book and the reception it had, see C. C. Adams, *Islam and Modernism in Egypt : A Study of the Modern Reform Movement Inaugurated by Muhammad Abduh*, Oxford University Press, 1933, pp. 259–65. For an analysis of the political forces behind the scenes, see Kedourie, loc. cit., p. 223 ff. For a French translation of the book, see *Revue des Etudes Islamiques* (*REI*), vols. VII and VIII, 1933 and 1934, pp. 353–91, and 163–232, and for an analysis of the judgment, see L. Bercher, *REI*, vol. IX, 1935, pp. 75–86.

36. About the 'Alī Brothers, see Sir Evan Cotton, ' Some Outstanding Political Leaders ' in *Political India*, ed. Sir John Cumming, London, 1932, pp. 199–201. See also Muhammad Ali, *For India and Islam*, Calcutta, 1922, where he explains his position *vis-à-vis* Gandhi's policy of non-aggression but adds that he cannot see how as loyal Muslims the Indians can compromise on the question of the Caliphate. He therefore denounces Ḥusayn and Fayṣal for disloyalty to the Caliph and for letting Islam down. See also W. G. Watson, *Muhammad Ali and the Khilafat Movement*, McGill University, M.A. thesis, 1955. Abu'l Kalām Āzād's autobiography, *India Wins Freedom*, London, 1959, was published posthumously; in

pp. 6–12 he tells very sketchily how he became a revolutionary and joined the Khilāfatists. Rashīd Riḍā published an Arabic translation from the Urdu of his *Kitāb al-Khilāfa al-Islāmiyya*, in *al-Manār*, vol. XXXIII, 1922, pp. 45–61 and 102–13, in which Abu'l Kalām Āzād concludes that all Caliphates after that of the Rāshidūn were purely temporal governments; there was a praiseworthy although slight return to this Caliphate with the advent of the Young Turks and the constitutional government of Abdul Ḥamīd because, as he explains, it practised consultation, Shūra, which is the first condition and the main characteristic of true Islamic government.

37. Toynbee, op. cit., pp. 56–9; for the text of this, see pp. 571–2. The Agha Khan published his memoirs in London in 1954 under the title *World Enough and Time*. On Amīr 'Alī, see article in *Encyclopaedia of Islam*, 2nd ed.

38. Toynbee, op. cit., p. 82; the full text of this statement is translated into French in *RMM*, vol. 64, 1926, pp. 29–33. Toynbee also gives the English translation, op. cit., pp. 576–8; Italian text can be had in *Oriente Moderno*, vol. IV, 1924, pp. 223–6.

39. Toynbee, op. cit., pp. 82–91. A *compte rendu* of the congress is given in *RMM*, vol. 64, 1926, pp. 3–122; in *RMM*, vol. 59, 1925, pp. 273–315, L. Massignon gives documents and bibliography on sovereignty and the Caliphate in Islam, and enumerates the attitudes of all the different contemporary parties on the Caliphate. Toynbee, op. cit., pp. 578–81, gives the English translation of *Memorandum submitted by the Third Committee of the Caliphate Congress held at Cairo on the 13th to 19th May, 1926* of the text taken from *Oriente Moderno*, vol. VI, pp. 272–3, and *RMM*, 1926, vol. 64, pp. 105–9.

40. Kedourie, loc. cit., p. 215 ff.; 'Abd ur-Raḥmān ar-Rafi'ī, *Muqaddimāt Thaurat 23 Yūlyu 1952*, Cairo, 1957, pp. 134–5.

INDEX